Garden Traditions

Member Recipes

Garden Traditions

Member Recipes

National Home Gardening Club
Minneapolis, Minnesota

Acknowledgements

We would like to thank NHGC members for sending us their favorite garden-fresh recipes as the foundation for *Garden Traditions: Member Recipes.*

Tom Carpenter
Creative Director

Michele Teigen
Senior Book Development Coordinator

Gina Germ
Photo Editor

David Farr & Jean Cook
ImageSmythe
Design and Production

Robin Krause
Food Stylist/Recipe Consultant

Jeff Johnson
Photography

Printed in 2007.

Photo Credits

William D. Adams pp. 38, 51, 57, 61, 79, 91, 107, 133, 135; Jim Block pp. 8 Both, 21, 23T, 30, 47, 52, 64, 85, 103, 106, 110, 123; Envision-George Mattei pp. 5, 33L, 78L, 89, 140T, 143, 147; Paul Poplis pp. 14, 34; Steven Needham pp. 17, 39, 44, 50, 70, 111, 121, 125, 128T, 139; Zeva Oelbaum pp. 28, 105, 115, 137R, 146; B.W. Hoffmann p. 32; Amy Reichman p. 37; Overseas p. 71L; Frank LaBua p. 82L; MAK p. 87; Daryl J. Solomon pp. 116, 124; Emily Johnson p. 122; PO London p. 133L; Dennis Galante p. 136; Saxon Holt pp. 13, 100, 113, 130, 131, 137L; Jeff Johnson pp. i, 1, 2-3, 4, 6, 9, 10, 15, 16, 19, 23, 24-25, 27, 29, 31, 33R, 35, 36, 40, 42, 43, 45, 46, 48-49, 53, 54, 56, 58, 60, 62-63, 66, 69, 72, 73, 75, 76-77, 78, 80, 81, 82R, 84, 86, 88, 90, 92, 93, 96, 97, 98-99, 101, 102, 104, 108, 109, 111, 112, 114, 118, 120, 123L, 126 Both, 127, 128B, 129, 132, 134, 138, 140B, 141, 142, 145; The Stock Market-John Curtis pp. ii-iii; F.B. Grunzweig/Photo Researchers p. 71; Photodisc Inc. p. 117; The Stock Market-Don Mason pp. 12, 74; Wes Thompson p. 26; Roy Morsch pp. 55, 59; Oddo & Sinibaldi p. 65; Peter Steiner p. 67; David Frazier p. 68; Bruce Peebles p. 83; Todd Haiman p. 94; Jean Miele p. 95; Bryan Peterson p. 144.

ISBN 10: 1–58159–011–3
ISBN 13: 978-1-58159–011–1
©1998 National Home Gardening Club
8 9 10 / 09 08 07

National Home Gardening Club
12301 Whitewater Drive
Minnetonka, MN 55343
www.gardeningclub.com

Table of Contents

Chapter 6 **Side Dishes, 76**

Chapter 7 **Main Dishes, 98**

Chapter 8 **Desserts, 118**

Enjoy the Bounty of Members' Favorite Recipe Traditions!

Think for a moment about one of your favorite recipes. Just what makes it so special?

Fresh, wholesome ingredients (like those you grow in your own garden) make a difference. So does good preparation, and cooking techniques that enhance the natural flavor of produce, fruit and other bounties of the land. Beautiful-looking accompaniments and garnishes also do wonders for any dish's appetite appeal.

But at the heart of any favorite recipe is the idea. Maybe that idea originated from an old, tattered magazine or newspaper clipping. Or, the well-used pages of an old favorite cookbook may have been the original seed for a recipe you now love. Often the best recipes are the ones handed down from generation to generation on note cards or pieces of notepaper stored in old recipe boxes. Some of the very best recipes are written down only in people's minds.

These are the kinds of ideas you'll find in this NHGC cookbook—*Garden Traditions: Member Recipes*. Here are hundreds of recipe ideas that make the most of your garden's harvest, and the harvest you get at any farmers' market or produce section.

These recipes also offer up a piece of each person kind enough to share their idea—a personal, time-honored tradition that has been tweaked and fine-tuned, sometimes for generations.

We thank every member who shared ideas, whether they made it into this volume or were slotted for future uses. It truly is the Member that makes the NHGC—and this book of recipe traditions—so special.

Enjoy the bounty!

Appetizers

Jalapeño-Cranberry Spread

Roast a variety of medium-spiced chili peppers: Anaheim, poblano or banana peppers. This spread goes great on these roasted peppers as well as with crackers.

4 fresh jalapeño peppers
2 cups fresh or frozen cranberries
2/3 cup sugar
2 (8-oz.) pkgs. cream cheese, softened
Favorite crackers

Scrape seeds out of peppers and discard. Chop peppers in food processor. Add cranberries and sugar. Process until coarsely chopped. Add cream cheese. Blend well. Serve spread with crackers.

David Thielbar
Grants Pass, OR

appetizers

relishes

salads

soups

breads

side dishes

main dishes

desserts

Great First Impression Stuffed Tomatoes

Stuff red, yellow or orange varieties of cherry tomatoes for an extra-appealing look.

12 oz. fresh mushrooms, sliced
1 small onion, finely chopped
1 clove garlic, minced
2 T. butter
1 cup pecan pieces
2 tsp. chopped, fresh thyme or ½ tsp. dried thyme leaves
Dash of ground nutmeg
Salt and pepper to taste
50 cherry tomatoes

In skillet, sauté mushrooms, onion and garlic in butter until tender. Place in food processor or blender with remaining ingredients, except tomatoes. Blend until smooth. Chill mixture. Cut tops off tomatoes and scoop out insides. Just prior to serving, stuff tomatoes with mushroom mixture.

Hint Serve any extra mushroom mixture with crackers.

Cassandra Vallianos
Astoria, NY

Zippy Cheese Log

Garnish this cheese log with sugar glazed berries: raspberries, blackberries and blueberries in the summer; cranberries in the winter.

2 (8-oz.) pkgs. cream cheese, softened
1 cup cottage cheese
1 envelope Italian salad dressing mix
¼ cup chopped, fresh parsley
½ cup chopped, cooked ham
½ cup chopped nuts

Thoroughly blend cheeses with dressing mix. Pat mixture into a ½-inch-thick rectangle (about 12 x 9 inches) on a wax-paper-lined baking sheet. Chill for 30 minutes in freezer or 1 hour in refrigerator, until firm.

Spread half of the parsley on 1 inch of long side of rectangle. Sprinkle ham over remaining rectangle. Beginning with the parsley edge, roll up tightly like a jelly roll, using a spatula to loosen cheese from wax paper while rolling. Combine nuts and remaining parsley, then sprinkle over roll to cover. Wrap roll in wax paper and chill overnight. Serve as a spread with crackers.

Ruth Knol
Annville, PA

Judy's Sugar Spice Pecans

These pecans make a great snack, or try sprinkling them on roasted squash or sweet potatoes.

1 T. butter
¾ cup sugar
2 tsp. pumpkin pie spice
1 tsp. ground cinnamon
½ tsp. salt
1 egg white
2 T. water
6 cups pecan halves

Heat oven to 275°F. Spread butter on cookie sheet. Combine sugar, spices and salt in large bowl. In second bowl, beat egg white and water together. Add pecans, 2 cups at a time, to egg white mixture, stirring to coat evenly. Transfer nuts to sugar-spice mixture. Repeat with remaining pecans until all 6 cups are in sugar-spice mixture. Stir until all pecans are coated.

Spread pecans on buttered cookie sheet. Bake for 20 minutes. Turn off heat and leave pecans in oven for 1 hour. Stir pecans and leave in oven until cool. (I leave mine in the oven overnight.) Store in airtight container.

Note As a substitute for pumpkin pie spice, use 1 tsp. ground cinnamon, ¼ tsp. ground cloves, ¼ tsp. ground nutmeg, ¼ tsp. ground ginger and ¼ tsp. ground allspice.

Elizabeth Everitt
Lake Elmo, MN

Deviled Eggs

Pack these eggs in an egg carton to take to a picnic or potluck.

6 large eggs, hard boiled
3¾ oz. sun-dried tomatoes packed in oil, drained and minced
¼ cup mayonnaise
3 T. sour cream
½ tsp. white wine vinegar
Salt and small pinch of cayenne pepper to taste
Fresh parsley, finely chopped for garnish

Halve the hard-boiled eggs lengthwise. Force the yolks through a strainer into a bowl. In the same bowl, stir in the minced tomatoes, mayonnaise, sour cream, vinegar, salt and pepper. Spoon the filling into the egg halves equally. Garnish the stuffed eggs with chopped parsley. Yields 6 to 12 servings.

Elaine Millsaps
Tampa, FL

Zucchini Appetizers

Cut these appetizers into larger pieces and serve warm with a garden salad for brunch or lunch.

3 cups zucchini, thinly sliced
  and unpared
½ cup vegetable oil
4 eggs, slightly beaten
1 cup Bisquick baking mix
½ cup finely chopped onion
½ cup Parmesan cheese
2 T. snipped parsley
½ tsp. salt
½ tsp. seasoned salt
½ tsp. dried oregano
Dash of pepper
1 large clove garlic, finely chopped

Heat oven to 350°F. Grease 9 x 13-inch baking dish. Mix wet and dry ingredients separately; then mix together thoroughly. Pour mixture into baking dish. Bake until golden brown, about 25 minutes. Cut into pieces, about 2 x 1-inch each. Serve warm or cold. Yields 4 dozen appetizers or 6 entree size servings.

This recipe freezes well and may be reheated in a microwave oven. It makes a delicious entree served hot with a garden salad for luncheons.

Bettye Pinter
Murfreesboro, TN

Hot Crab Sandwich

Slice each muffin in half and serve as an appetizer with cucumber slices. These sandwiches are perfect for quick snacks and suppers, too.

1¼ lbs. king crab meat, chunked
1¼ cups mayonnaise
2 green onions, chopped
½ head of lettuce, chopped
1 T. salt
½ tsp. lemon juice
12 tomato slices
6 English muffins, sliced and toasted
12 slices mozzarella cheese

Heat oven to 350°F. Mix crab meat with mayonnaise, onions, lettuce, salt and lemon juice. Place a tomato slice on each muffin. Arrange crab mixture on top of tomato. Top with cheese. Bake until lightly brown, about 5 to 7 minutes.

Betty Lou Cordi
Barton, NY

Vegetable Pizza

Garden-fresh vegetables make this appetizer pizza full of flavor and beautiful to behold.

2 cans refrigerated crescent rolls
2 (8-oz.) pkgs. cream cheese, softened
1 cup salad dressing or mayonnaise
1 T. chopped, fresh dillweed or 1 tsp. dried dillweed
1 tsp. garlic powder

Toppings
Green bell pepper, sliced or chopped
Carrots, sliced or shredded
Broccoli florets
Cauliflower florets
Tomatoes, sliced or chopped
Cheddar cheese, shredded

Spread crescent rolls in bottom of baking pan or on cookie sheet. Bake as directed on package. Combine cream cheese, salad dressing, dillweed and garlic powder. Spread mixture over baked crust. Top with desired toppings. Cut into small pieces for appetizers.

Debbie Kirsch
Harbor Beach, MI

Spicy Mushrooms

Mushroom caps and the spicy pepperoni mixture combine to create a wonderful taste.

30 medium to large button mushrooms
2 T. butter
1 medium onion, finely chopped
8 oz. pepperoni, finely chopped
1/3 cup finely chopped, green bell pepper
1 clove garlic, minced
1/2 cup finely crushed Ritz crackers
3 T. grated fresh Parmesan cheese
1 T. finely chopped, fresh parsley
1/2 tsp. seasoned salt
1/4 tsp. dried oregano leaves
1/8 tsp. freshly ground pepper
1/3 cup chicken broth

Heat oven to 325°F. Clean mushrooms. Remove stems and set caps aside. Finely chop stems. Melt butter in skillet over medium heat. Add mushroom stems, onion, pepperoni, green pepper and garlic. Sauté until vegetables are tender but not brown. Add crackers, cheese, parsley, salt, oregano and pepper. Mix well. Stir in chicken broth. Remove from heat.

Spoon stuffing mixture into reserved mushroom caps. Place caps in well-buttered shallow baking dish. Add water to just cover the bottom of baking dish (about 1/8 inch deep). Bake uncovered for 25 minutes.

Cynthia Cernauskas
Valparaiso, IN

Salmon Spread

**Fresh herbs of dill, fennel, mint or borage look beautiful wrapped around
this salmon appetizer. Serve it with crackers or garden peas, beans and cucumbers.**

8 oz. smoked salmon
8-oz. pkg. cream cheese, softened
2 T. chopped, fresh garlic chives
1 T. grated onion
1 T. horseradish
1 T. lemon juice
Pepper to taste
Chopped, fresh parsley or
  other herb

Combine all ingredients, except parsley, mixing until smooth. Shape mixture into a ball or log and roll in chopped parsley or other herbs. Serve as a spread with crackers.

*Colleen Wolling
Savannah, GA*

Chapter 2

Relishes

Zucchini Relish

During the canning season, invite your friends over and have them each bring their favorite relish recipe and its ingredients. Then prepare the recipes together, and fill your pantry with jars of summer.

10 cups chopped zucchini
4 cups chopped onions
3 green bell peppers, seeded
2 red bell peppers, seeded
5 tsp. salt
5 cups sugar
2¼ cups apple cider vinegar
2 tsp. cornstarch
2 tsp. celery seed
1 tsp. ground mustard
1 tsp. ground turmeric

Grind the zucchini, onions and bell peppers. Sprinkle mixture with salt and let stand overnight. Rinse and drain. In a large pot, combine vegetable mixture with remaining ingredients. Bring to a boil. Reduce heat. Simmer, uncovered, for 30 minutes. Seal relish in hot jars.

Dennis Eyzabroad
Starks, LA

appetizers

relishes

salads

soups

breads

side
dishes

main
dishes

desserts

Simple Southwest Salsa

This is a quick salsa to prepare for chips or to serve with fish or chicken.

4 to 5 Roma tomatoes
½ medium green bell pepper
½ medium onion (or 2 to 4 green onions)
Juice of ½ lime
2 to 4 sprigs fresh oregano, snipped
    (or 1 T. dried oregano leaves)

Cut tomatoes lengthwise and remove seeds. Cut each half into 8 wedges, then slice crosswise, making a small dice. Chop pepper and onion. Toss tomatoes, onion and pepper together with lime juice. Sprinkle with oregano and mix well. Chill. Serve with corn chips or your favorite chips.

Thella Brock
St. George, UT

Green Tomato Relish

Serve this relish on turkey and ham sandwiches. Tuck a couple of slices of ripe tomato in the sandwich for even more garden flavor.

4 cups chopped green tomatoes
3 cups chopped green cabbage
3 green bell peppers, seeded and chopped
2 red bell peppers, seeded and chopped
1 large onion, finely chopped
2 T. pickling salt
1¼ cups sugar
1¼ cups cider vinegar
½ cup water
2 tsp. mustard seed
1 tsp. celery seed
½ tsp. ground turmeric

Place all vegetables in large bowl and sprinkle with the salt. Stir well, cover and refrigerate overnight. Rinse vegetables well and drain in colander.

In large pot, combine remaining ingredients. Bring to a boil, stirring to dissolve sugar. Stir in vegetables and return to a boil. Remove from heat. Ladle hot relish into hot, sterilized jars, leaving ½ inch of head space. Wipe jar rims and adjust lids. Process in boiling water canner for 5 minutes for half pints or 10 minutes for pints.

Note This recipe makes 3 to 4 pints.

JoAnn Stearns
Custer, SD

Salsa

This salsa uses a variety of vine-ripened tomatoes, and makes a great accompaniment to black beans and corn chips.

2 lbs. "juicy" tomatoes (Big Boy, Early Girl or Beefsteak)

3 lbs. "meaty" tomatoes (Roma, Pear, Jubilee)

2 large yellow onions, coarsely chopped

2 large yellow bell peppers, seeded and coarsely chopped

1 large green bell pepper, seeded and coarsely chopped

10 jalapeño peppers, coarsely chopped

2 habanero peppers, finely chopped

$\frac{1}{4}$ cup coarsely chopped fresh parsley

$\frac{1}{4}$ cup lemon juice

2 tsp. white vinegar

Dried oregano leaves to taste

Freshly ground pepper to taste

Blanch and peel tomatoes. Core and squeeze them to remove seeds and excess liquid, then coarsely chop them. Combine all ingredients in a large pot. Bring to a boil. Reduce heat. Simmer, uncovered, until desired thickness. (Cornstarch may be added to assist thickening and add a glossy appearance.) Let salsa cool and pour into freezer-safe containers and freeze. Salsa may also be canned, if desired.

Noelle Travis
Cedar Rapids, IA

Corncob Jelly

This unique jelly offers hints of apple jelly. Serve on toast and use it to brush on pie crusts and tarts before adding the fruit.

12 cups bright red corn cobs
(from field corn), broken
3 cups water

1.75-oz. pkg. fruit pectin (Sure-Jell)
3 cups sugar

Boil cobs in 6 cups water for 30 minutes. Remove from heat. Strain the liquid. Add enough water to bring liquid level back to 3 cups, if necessary. Add fruit pectin. Bring to a rolling boil. Stir in sugar and boil for 2 to 3 minutes or until mixture "sheets" from the spoon (this is the jelly stage on a candy thermometer).

Dolores Broberg
Shelton, WA

Crispy Sweet Crispy Pickles

These microwave pickles are ready to eat as soon as they are well chilled.

½ cup sugar
½ cup white vinegar
½ tsp. salt
¼ tsp. celery seed
¼ tsp. ground turmeric
¼ tsp. mustard seed
2 cucumbers, unpeeled, thinly sliced
2 red or white onions, thinly sliced

In microwave-safe bowl or large measuring cup, combine sugar, vinegar, salt, celery seed. turmeric and mustard seed. Add cucumbers and onions. Stir until vegetables are covered. Microwave, uncovered, on high power for 5 minutes. Stir. Microwave on high for 5 minutes longer. Pour mixture into quart jar and refrigerate.

Tiena Parsons
Andover, KS

Lemon-Herb Dressing

Serve this wonderful herb dressing over fresh-picked salad greens from your garden or the farmers' market.

½ cup olive oil
2 T. lemon juice
2 small cloves
 garlic, minced
1 tsp. dried
 oregano leaves
1 tsp. dried basil
 leaves
1 tsp. salt
¼ tsp. pepper

Combine all ingredients in a jar and shake until well blended.

Kimberly Young Windber, PA

Cinnamon Basil Jelly

Try this jelly with a simple antipasto supper of dry salami, roasted peppers, piquant cheeses and dark rye bread.

1¾ cups cinnamon basil infusion
    (1½ cups cinnamon basil, including leaves and stems
    and 2¼ cups of water—see instructions below)
2 T. lemon juice
3½ cups sugar
1 pouch liquid Certo

Make the infusion by simmering the cinnamon basil and water for 10 minutes. Strain and measure an exact amount (1¾ cups) into a new saucepan. Add lemon juice and sugar. Stir over medium heat until sugar dissolves and mixture comes to a boil; then immediately add Certo. Bring back to a boil, stirring constantly; then remove from heat. Pour into processed, sterilized jars and seal. Yields five 8-ounce jars.

Darlene Keith
Manchester, CT

Squash Pickles

Make these pickles with sliced yellow squash, or pattypan squash you have cut in half.

8 cups thinly sliced yellow squash
2 cups thinly sliced yellow onions
Salt
4 green bell peppers, seeded and chopped
3 cups sugar
2 cups white vinegar
2 tsp. celery seed
2 tsp. mustard seed
1 tsp. ground turmeric

Combine squash and onions. Sprinkle generously with salt and set aside for 1 hour. Drain. Combine peppers, sugar, vinegar, celery seed, mustard seed and turmeric in a large pot. Bring to a boil. Add squash and onions. Return to a boil. Pack mixture into sterilized pint jars and seal.

Nancy Sparagowski
Crestview, FL

Chokecherry Jelly

Although chokecherries don't make great out-of-hand eating, they make exquisite jams and jellies like this.

3 cups chokecherry juice
6½ cups sugar
1 bottle liquid fruit pectin (or 2 packs dry fruit pectin)
¼ tsp. almond extract (optional)

In a large kettle, combine juice and sugar. Stir to mix. Bring to a boil over high heat, stirring constantly. Stir in pectin. Return to a rolling boil and boil for 1 minute more, stirring constantly. Remove from heat. Stir and skim off foam for 5 minutes. Add almond extract. Seal in hot jars.

Note To make chokecherry syrup, omit the pectin. Family and friends will love this wonderful syrup on pancakes or over ice cream.

Della Melling
Alba, MI

Green Tomato Mincemeat

This delicious filling is perfect for pies and tarts.
The traditional service is with ham, turkey or roast pork.

3 qts. finely chopped green tomatoes
3 qts. finely chopped, unpeeled apples
1 lb. seedless raisins
5 cups light brown sugar
¾ cup white vinegar
½ cup lemon juice
½ cup water
2 T. grated orange peel
2 T. grated lemon peel
1 T. ground cinnamon
2 tsp. salt
¼ tsp. ground cloves
¼ tsp. ground allspice

Combine all ingredients in a large kettle. Bring to a boil, stirring frequently. Reduce heat and simmer until mixture is dark and thick, stirring occasionally (about 2 hours). Pour hot mixture into quart jars. Adjust lids and process in boiling water bath canner for 25 minutes.

Anita King
Greenwich, NY

Artificial Honey

This beautiful and flavorful "honey" is a natural on toast and biscuits.

5 lbs. sugar
3 cups water
Alum, a piece the size of a cherry
12 red rose petals, unsprayed and
    rinsed in cold water
8 pink rose petals, unsprayed and
    rinsed in cold water
20 white clover blossoms, unsprayed
    and rinsed in cold water

Combine sugar and water in saucepan. Bring to a boil, stirring until sugar is dissolved. Add alum and boil for 2 minutes. Remove from heat and add rose petals and clover blossoms. Let stand for 10 minutes. Strain into sterilized jelly jars and seal with melted paraffin wax.

Dolores Broberg
Shelton, WA

Refrigerated Pickled Zucchini

Cut the zucchini into slices with a crinkle cutter for an interesting shape. For extra variety, cut the zucchini into thin "matchsticks."

1 T. pickling spices
1 cup sugar
1 cup white vinegar
1 cup water
2 medium zucchini, thinly sliced
1 onion, thinly sliced

Place spices in a cheesecloth pouch. In a saucepan, combine sugar, vinegar, water and spice pouch. Bring to a boil, stirring to dissolve sugar. Remove from heat. Layer zucchini and onion in large jar or container with a lid. Pour vinegar mixture over top. Cool. Refrigerate for several days before eating.

Lucile Edelbrock
Richmond, MN

Salsa Fresca

Look for any unusual and pretty tortilla chips, like blue corn dusted with cayenne powder or sesame seeds, to go with this fresh salsa.

1 large ripe tomato (about ¾ lb.)
2 large tomatillos (about 6 oz. total)
¼ cup fresh cilantro, chopped
⅓ cup onion or green onions, chopped

2 T. lime juice (or lemon juice or 4 T. red wine vinegar)
2 to 6 T. fresh or canned hot chilies or jalapeños, minced
Salt

Core and coarsely chop tomato. Husk and chop tomatillos. Combine these with other ingredients and salt to taste. Serve with tortilla chips. Yields 2½ to 3 cups.

Note A tomatillo resembles a small green tomato, except that the skin is thin and parchment-like.

Esther Tikalsky
Belle Plaine, MN

"Raspberry" Jam

Prepare this with different flavors of gelatin mixes to make many varieties of jam.

5 cups puréed green tomatoes
4 cups sugar
6-oz. pkg. raspberry-flavored gelatin mix
3 tsp. lemon juice

Combine tomato purée and sugar in a saucepan. Boil for 15 minutes, stirring until sugar is dissolved. Add gelatin and lemon juice. Boil for 5 minutes longer. Skim foam from top. Pour jam into sterilized jars and can as usual or freeze.

Denise Wojciechowski
Fraser, MI

Grandma's Pickled Green Tomatoes

These pickled tomatoes are the perfect go-along relish for family camping trips.

Wash green tomatoes. If they are too large to fit into a quart jar, quarter them. Fit the tomatoes into place in the jars. Add the following ingredients to each jar:

1 T. pickling spice
1 T. salt
¼ cup vinegar
Fresh sprigs of dill
Fresh sprig of summer savory
3 cloves of garlic

Fill each jar with cold water to within ¼ inch of jar top. Seal for 6 weeks. Turn jars each week. These pickled green tomatoes are great with toasted cheese sandwiches!

Pamela Viera
Garfield Heights, OH

Okra Pickles

Decorate a bed of mixed organic greens with these okra pickles, some julienned red peppers and creamy gorgonzola.

3½ lbs. small okra pods
4 to 5 small hot peppers
4 to 5 garlic cloves
1 pint distilled white vinegar
1 quart water
½ cup salt
2 tsp. dill seeds

Pack okra firmly in hot, sterilized ball jars. Put a garlic clove and hot pepper in each jar. Mix vinegar, water, salt and dill seeds in a large saucepan and bring to a boil. Pour boiling brine in jars and seal. Process in boiling water bath at simmering temperature about 180 to 200°F for 10 minutes. Let ripen several weeks before opening. Yields 4 to 5 pints.

Norma Parks
Deepwater, MO

Chapter 3

Salads

Shrimp and Summer Vegetable Salad

Serve this salad on a bed of your favorite greens. Watercress, arugula and mâche make a great combination.

2 cups cooked cocktail shrimp
2 medium tomatoes, seeded and diced
1 cup diced baby zucchini
1 cup diced baby yellow summer squash
½ cup diced, seeded cucumber
¼ cup diced red onion
1 tsp. minced garlic
8-oz. bottle Italian dressing
Lettuce of choice
Croutons (optional)
Grated Parmesan cheese (optional)

Combine shrimp, all vegetables and garlic in a salad bowl. Pour dressing over top and toss to combine. Refrigerate for 1 hour, stirring once or twice. Serve on bed of lettuce with croutons and Parmesan cheese, if desired.

Sheryl Vigue
Dexter, ME

appetizers

relishes

salads

soups

breads

side
dishes

main
dishes

desserts

Fruit Fancy for 12

Add varieties of mint leaves or lemon balm to this lovely fruit salad. About 2 tablespoons of chopped, fresh mint will season the fruit nicely.

½ cup sugar
2 T. cornstarch
20-oz. can pineapple (chunks or tidbits),
   drained (reserve juice)
1 tsp. grated orange peel
⅓ cup fresh orange juice

1 T. lemon juice
11-oz. can mandarin oranges, drained
2 (or more) bananas, sliced
2 medium apples, cored and chopped
Seedless green grapes
Strawberries

Combine sugar and cornstarch in medium saucepan. Blend in reserved pineapple juice, orange peel, orange juice and lemon juice. Cook over medium heat until mixture boils and thickens, stirring constantly. Boil and stir for 1 minute. Combine remaining ingredients in a large bowl. Pour hot sauce over fruit and stir to coat. Refrigerate overnight.

Karen Grimm
Cologne, MN

Delicious Potato Salad

The splash of vinegar adds to the dressing. Try adding tarragon, nasturtium or lemon thyme to the vinegar and sample it in this interesting salad.

Salad
12 cups shredded, cooked potatoes
12 hard-cooked eggs, chopped
1½ cups chopped celery
½ medium onion, chopped

Dressing
3 cups salad dressing or mayonnaise
2 cups sugar
½ cup sour cream
2 T. mustard
2 tsp. salt
Vinegar to taste (optional)

In a large bowl, combine potatoes, eggs, celery and onion. Combine all dressing ingredients; mix well. Add dressing to salad. Stir gently to combine.

Mrs. Jerry Miller
Dundee, OH

Shimmery Blueberry Salad

Your choice of red wine will drive the flavor of this salad. Select from Red Zinfandel, Pinot Noir or Merlot. For a refreshing variation, make this salad with ginger ale instead of wine.

1½ cups boiling water
⅓ cup sugar
2 envelopes unflavored gelatin
2 cups fruity red wine
2 cups fresh blueberries
11-oz. can mandarin oranges, drained

Dissolve sugar and gelatin in boiling water. Stir in wine. Refrigerate until it is as thick as unbeaten egg whites, stirring occasionally. Fold in blueberries and oranges. Spoon into mold, and refrigerate for 4 hours or until set.

Marcella West (Moore)
Washington, IL

Beet and Herring Salad

Match this treat with field greens and crusty bread for a superb summer meal.

5 medium beets, tops removed
2 apples, peeled and cored
   (any variety that is not too tart)
4 hard-cooked eggs, peeled
2 dill pickles
1 potato, peeled and boiled
½ to ⅔ lb. pickled herring, drained
⅓ cup pickle juice
3 T. mayonnaise
3 T. yellow prepared mustard
1 T. Worcestershire sauce

Cook beets in boiling water until easily pierced with a fork. Let cool. Peel beets. (Skins will easily scrape off with a knife.) Using the shredding side of a grater, grate beets, apples, eggs, pickles and potato into a large bowl. Add remaining ingredients. Fold all together. (Do not stir or mixture will become too mushy.) Chill salad for at least 1 hour. Serve with slices of French bread. Salad will last no more than one week in the refrigerator.

Christy Harshbarger
Spokane, WA

Garden Tabbouleh

Try adding the petals of edible flowers, which have a spiced pepper flavor, to accent the grain in this salad.

½ cup dry bulgur
½ cup plus 2 T. boiling water
½ cup fresh parsley, chopped
¼ cup onion, chopped
1 to 2 tomatoes, cubed
¼ cup fresh lemon juice
¼ cup olive oil
Salt to taste
½ cup mixture of your favorite raw
  vegetables
Petals of 6 edible flowers, calendula,
  nasturtium or sunflower

Add dry bulgur to boiling water. Remove from heat, cover and set aside for 10 minutes. The water should be absorbed and the kernels swelled. You will have approximately 1 cup of prepared bulgur. Add parsley, onion, tomatoes, lemon juice, olive oil and salt to prepared bulgur. Mix well and chill for 1 hour. Add your selection of garden vegetables just before serving.

Susan Cunic
Pikeville, TN

Sauerkraut Salad

For even more flavor, chop a chili pepper into this salad.

16-oz. can or bag of sauerkraut,
    drained
1 cup grated carrots
1 cup chopped celery
1 cup chopped green bell pepper
1 cup chopped onion
4-oz. jar diced pimientos, drained
¾ cup sugar
½ cup vegetable oil
2 T. white vinegar

In a large bowl, combine sauerkraut, carrots, celery, green pepper, onion and pimientos. In a jar or small bowl, combine sugar, oil and vinegar. Shake or whisk until dressing has creamy consistency. Pour dressing over vegetables and mix well. Cover and refrigerate for at least 8 hours.

Hint This salad can be made a day or two ahead of when you want it. It keeps well in the refrigerator.

Betty Megdall
Livonia, MI

Pasta and Cucumber Salad

This salad is delicious accompanying poached, fresh salmon.

1 lb. pasta (such as mostaccioli, large shells, pipe rigatoni)
Vegetable oil
1 white onion, diced
1 cucumber, unpeeled, thinly sliced and quartered
½ cup sugar
½ cup white vinegar
1 tsp. salt
1 tsp. pepper
1 tsp. garlic powder
2 T. dried parsley
1 jar chopped pimiento or ½ red pepper, chopped

Cook pasta in salt water according to package directions. Drain. In bowl, coat pasta well with oil. Add onion and cucumber. In a separate bowl, combine the sugar, vinegar, salt, pepper, garlic powder, parsley and pimiento. Stir ingredients together and pour over pasta mixture. Toss. Chill in refrigerator for at least 2 hours before serving. Toss again before serving. Yields 12 to 15 servings.

Alice M. Davis
Siloam Springs, AR

Renee's Awesome Spinach Salad

The caramelized almonds in this recipe add delicious flavor.

Dressing
½ cup sugar
½ cup vegetable oil
¼ cup apple cider vinegar
2 T. sesame seeds
1½ T. grated onion
1 T. poppy seeds
¼ tsp. paprika
¼ tsp. Worcestershire sauce
Cayenne to taste

Almond Mix
½ cup sliced almonds
Sugar

Salad
1 bundle fresh spinach, cleaned and trimmed
2 to 3 Satsuma oranges (or canned mandarin oranges)
2 to 4 green onions, diced
1 to 2 ribs celery, diced

Blend all dressing ingredients until uniform consistency. Set aside. Place almonds in a skillet and lightly coat with sugar (don't be too shy). Cook over medium-low heat until sugar starts to melt, stirring constantly. Cook and stir until sugar is almost caramelized. (You may add more sugar as the almonds cook.) Cool.

In a large bowl, combine salad ingredients (spinach, oranges, onions and celery) and almonds. Add dressing just before serving and toss to coat.

Renee DeFranz
Vancouver, WA

My Mom's Cranberry Salad

Make this salad with toasted walnuts, pecans, pistachios or hickory nuts.

1 small pkg. red gelatin
2 cups boiling water
1 cup sugar
1 cup crushed pineapple, drained
  (reserve 1 cup juice)
2 cups chopped cranberries
1 cup chopped celery
1 cup chopped nuts
1 orange, peeled and chopped

Dissolve gelatin in boiling water. Add sugar and stir until dissolved. Add juice from pineapple. (If you don't have 1 cup juice, add water to juice to equal 1 cup.) Refrigerate until mixture is the consistency of egg white. Add cranberries, celery, nuts and orange. Pour into mold and chill until set. Unmold when ready to serve.

Note For better chopping, freeze the cranberries whole and freeze the orange cut into eighths, then use a blender or food processor to chop them.

Dianne Replogle
Poland, OH

Sweet Potato Salad with Pecans

You can also make this delicious salad by roasting pieces of sweet potato in the oven with olive oil. There's no reason to peel the sweet potatoes; the skin provides many nutrients.

3 lbs. sweet potatoes
2 cups chopped celery
2 cups low-fat yogurt
1 cup chopped onion
1 cup low-fat mayonnaise
2 cloves garlic, minced
2 tsp. ground or freshly
   grated ginger
1 tsp. ground cinnamon
½ tsp. freshly grated nutmeg
1 lb. pecans, coarsely chopped
Whole pecans for garnishing salad

Bake sweet potatoes until tender. Peel potatoes, let cool, then coarsely dice them. Set potatoes aside. In a large mixing bowl, combine remaining ingredients, except pecans. Add chopped pecans and mix well. Add sweet potatoes and gently fold in. (Try to keep potatoes from getting mushy.) Decorate top of salad with whole pecans. Cover with plastic wrap. Refrigerate at least 2 hours or overnight.

Note To serve warm, bake in a 300°F oven for 30 minutes or less. Serve immediately.

Thomas Livers
Louisville, KY

Cucumber-Onion Salad

Serve this salad with a plate of sliced, ripened tomatoes.

2 cups white vinegar
¾ to 1½ cups sugar (to taste)
2½ T. salt
2 tsp. pepper
Cucumbers, peeled and sliced
Onion slices

Combine vinegar, sugar, salt and pepper. Stir to dissolve sugar. Add cucumbers and onion slices. Marinate vegetables for 15 minutes before serving.

Rose Boyer
Hecker, IL

Mexican Salad

Prepare this salad when tomatoes are ripe. Substitute cherry tomatoes for the seeded and diced tomatoes, if you wish.

1 head lettuce, chopped
1 medium onion, finely chopped
1 lb. mild cheddar cheese, shredded
1 cup shredded carrots
2 large tomatoes, seeded and diced
15-oz. can pinto beans, rinsed and
    drained
10.5-oz. bag corn chips, crushed
16-oz. bottle Catalina salad dressing

Combine lettuce, onion, cheese, carrots, tomatoes and beans in a large bowl. Mix well. Chill. Just before serving, add corn chips and dressing. Toss to coat. Serve immediately.

Nancy Sparagowski
Crestview, FL

Favorite Broccoli Salad

Sunflower seeds add a flavorful complement to this broccoli and cauliflower salad that is popular at picnics, parties and family gatherings.

Salad
1 bunch broccoli, separated into florets
1 head cauliflower, separated into florets
16-oz. pkg. bacon, fried, drained and crumbled
1 cup chopped tomatoes
1/4 cup sunflower seeds

Dressing
1 cup mayonnaise
1/3 cup sugar
1 T. apple cider vinegar

Combine broccoli, cauliflower, bacon, tomatoes and sunflower seeds in a large bowl. Whisk together dressing ingredients. Just before serving, pour dressing over salad and toss to coat.

*Gail Doll
Harvey, ND*

Fancy Chicken Salad

Roast a chicken with garlic, rosemary and thyme and use the leftovers for this salad.

1/2 cup mayonnaise
2 T. milk
1 T. lemon juice
1 tsp. salt
1/2 tsp. dry mustard
1/4 tsp. pepper
3 cups chopped, cooked chicken
2 1/2 cups halved, red seedless grapes
3/4 cup diced celery
3/4 cup cashews

Combine mayonnaise, milk, lemon juice, salt, mustard and pepper. Stir until smooth. Add chicken, grapes, celery and cashews. Toss well to combine and serve.

*Kathryn Nulph
Callery, PA*

Apple Harvest Salad

Add a sprinkling of nutmeg or cardamom to this salad. The spice can be folded into the whipped cream.

20-oz. can crushed pineapple, undrained
2/3 cup sugar
1 pkg. lemon-flavored gelatin
8-oz. pkg. cream cheese, softened
1 cup diced, unpeeled apples
1 cup chopped celery
1 cup whipped cream or whipped topping
1/2 cup chopped pecans

In a saucepan, combine pineapple and sugar. Bring to a boil, stirring to dissolve sugar. Boil for 3 minutes. Stir in gelatin until dissolved. Stir in cream cheese until well blended. Let cool, but do not let it set up.

After mixture has cooled, add apples, celery, whipped cream and nuts. Refrigerate until set.

Peggy Lee Payne
Lexington, VA

Pasta Pineapple Potato Salad

Prepare this salad with baby new potatoes and you will not need to peel the potatoes.

6 medium potatoes, peeled and diced
½ cup uncooked rotini pasta
3 T. olive oil, divided
1 large onion, chopped
4 sweet banana peppers, seeded and finely chopped
2 carrots, shredded
1 can crushed pineapple, undrained
½ cup sunflower seeds
½ cup mayonnaise
Pepper to taste

In a large saucepan, combine potatoes with enough water to cover. Bring water to a boil over high heat. Reduce heat to medium-high. Cook for 15 minutes, then add pasta and 1 tablespoon oil. Continue to cook until pasta is tender. Remove from heat. Drain, rinse with cold water and drain again.

In a heavy skillet, heat remaining 2 tablespoons oil over medium heat. Sauté onion and banana pepper in oil until onion is golden brown. Remove from heat. In a large bowl, combine onion mixture and carrots. Add pineapple, sunflower seeds, mayonnaise and pasta mixture, stirring after each addition. Add pepper to taste. Cover and chill for at least 2 hours.

Donald Hall
Hendersonville, NC

Cranberry Salad

Prepare this salad with orchard Haralson, Liberty or Fireside apples.

1 pkg. fresh cranberries
2 tart apples, cored
2 oranges (1 peeled and 1 unpeeled)
1 small can crushed pineapple, drained
2 cups sugar
½ cup chopped walnuts (optional)

Grind cranberries, apples and oranges in food grinder or food processor. Mix well with remaining ingredients. Refrigerate.

Hint This salad is best if made a day or two ahead of when you want to serve it.

Rita Hanson
South Shore, KY

Chicken Rice Salad

Give this salad different flavors by preparing it with different types of rice. Wild rice, jasmine and basmati are a few types to try.

5 cups cubed, cooked chicken
3 cups cooked rice
1½ cups diced green bell pepper
1½ cups sliced celery
20-oz. can pineapple tidbits, drained
¾ cup mayonnaise
4 tsp. orange juice
2 tsp. white vinegar
1 tsp. salt
½ tsp. ground ginger
¼ tsp. garlic salt
15-oz. can mandarin oranges, drained
1 cup slivered almonds, toasted

In a large bowl, combine chicken, rice, green pepper, celery and pineapple. In a small bowl, combine mayonnaise, orange juice, vinegar, salt, ginger and garlic salt. Add to chicken mixture and toss to coat. Chill. Just before serving, fold in the oranges and almonds.

Betty Mezdall
Livonia, MI

Vegetable Pasta Salad

Serve this pasta salad on a bed of tomato slices seasoned with fresh basil leaves and vinegar.

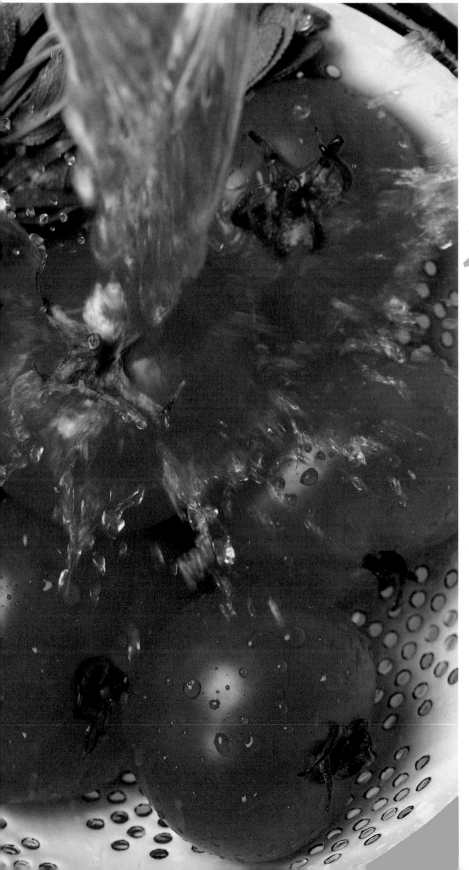

5 hard-cooked eggs
1 pkg. elbow macaroni, cooked and
    drained
2 large ripe tomatoes, diced
1 large green bell pepper, seeded
    and diced
1 cup diced celery
½ cup salad dressing or mayonnaise
4 green onions, sliced
⅛ tsp. salt
⅛ tsp. pepper

Discard egg yolks and dice the whites. In a large bowl, combine eggs and remaining ingredients. Stir gently to mix. Chill for at least 45 minutes.

John Glover
Trenton, TN

Southwestern Rice and Bean Salad

Blanch corn on the cob and cut the kernels off the cob to make this zesty salad.

2 cups cooked long-grain rice
16-oz. can kidney beans, rinsed and drained
8 ears fresh corn on the cob, blanched,
    kernels removed
½ cup sliced green onions with tops
½ cup picante sauce
¼ cup Italian dressing
1 tsp. ground cumin

Combine all ingredients in a large salad bowl. Cover and refrigerate for 2 to 3 hours or until chilled, stirring once or twice.

Betty Megdall
Livonia, MI

German Cucumber Salad

Vine-ripened cucumbers and tomatoes add a special touch to this salad.

2 medium cucumbers, thinly sliced
4 green onions, thinly sliced
3 small tomatoes, sliced
2 T. snipped, fresh parsley

Dressing

$\frac{1}{4}$ cup sour cream
2 T. snipped, fresh dill
1 T. white vinegar
1 T. milk
$\frac{1}{2}$ tsp. salt
$\frac{1}{4}$ tsp. prepared yellow mustard
$\frac{1}{8}$ tsp. pepper

In a bowl, combine cucumbers, onions, tomatoes and parsley. In a small bowl, combine dressing ingredients. Pour dressing over cucumber mixture and toss gently to combine. Cover and chill for at least 1 hour.

Betty Megdall
Livonia, MI

Creamed Cucumbers

Grate some red onion into this recipe for a splash of color.

$4\frac{1}{2}$ cups sliced cucumbers (peel, if desired)
1 cup sour cream
3 T. grated onion
2 T. white vinegar
1 T. sugar
$1\frac{1}{2}$ tsp. salt

Mix all ingredients well. Cover and chill for at least 2 hours.

Faye Lewis
Knoxville, TN

Veggie Macaroni Salad

This colorful confetti salad becomes even more beautiful when served in bright Depression glass or heirloom bowls.

2 lbs. macaroni noodles
1 T. butter or margarine
Mayonnaise to moisten
6 stalks of celery hearts, diced small
4 to 5 sweet pickles, chopped finely
6 medium fresh spring onions, chopped fine
2 6-inch fresh cucumbers, peeled and diced thin
10 fresh red radishes, diced small
2 fresh medium green bell peppers, diced small (or use 1 bell pepper
    and 2 banana peppers)
2 large fresh carrots, diced small
1 large fresh tomato, diced
Parsley, salt and pepper to taste

Cook noodles until firm but not overdone and drain. Stir noodles gently in bowl while adding the butter. While warm (not hot) add all remaining ingredients except the tomato, beginning with the mayonnaise. Gently add the tomato pieces and sprinkle the salad with parsley, salt and pepper, if desired. Refrigerate a few hours before serving. Yields 20 servings.

Tonna Evans
Street, MD

Fay's Lentil Salad

Make this recipe on a Saturday night and have a lazy Sunday afternoon with this satisfying salad and grilled lamb kabobs.

1 lb. dried lentils
5 cups water
2 tsp. salt
¾ cup olive oil
¼ cup red wine vinegar
1 large clove garlic, minced

¾ cup onions, chopped
1 tsp. coarse ground black pepper
½ tsp. Worcestershire sauce
¼ tsp. Tabasco or other hot sauce
Yellow and red peppers

Cook the lentils for 30 minutes in 5 cups of water containing 2 teaspoons of salt. Drain the lentils and add the olive oil while the lentils are still hot. Cool the lentil-oil mixture to room temperature. Mix in the remaining ingredients except for yellow and red peppers. Refrigerate the lentil salad overnight. When serving, garnish salad with slices of yellow and red peppers.

Ervin Hindin
Pullman, WA

Norwegian Red Sauerkraut

**Guests will love the look and taste of this salad; pair
it with game or other sausages and potato dumplings.**

1½ lbs. red cabbage, shredded
1 or 2 apples, cut in wedges
2 tsp. salt
1 tsp. caraway seeds
1 cup water
2 T. vinegar, plus additional vinegar to taste
2 T. sugar

Place cabbage, apples and seasonings in layers in a pan. Pour water and 2 tablespoons vinegar over top. Simmer covered about 30 to 45 minutes until cabbage and apples are tender. Add more water if necessary to keep sauerkraut from sticking. Before serving, season to taste with more vinegar and sugar if needed.

By adding the vinegar before simmering, the bright red color of the apples and cabbage is retained, and the dish is a beautiful addition to the holiday table.

Melody Rose
Benton, KY

salads

Wilted Spinach Salad

A nice substitute for bacon is to caramelize a sliced yellow onion in butter until sweet, mellow and golden brown.

4 cups spinach
2 T. sliced green onion
Dash of freshly ground
    pepper
2 slices bacon
2 T. vinegar
1 tsp. sugar
1 tsp. Dijon mustard
1 T. snipped, fresh tarragon
    or ½ tsp. dried tarragon
⅛ tsp. salt

Wash spinach; pat dry on paper towel. Tear spinach into pieces and place in bowl. Add green onion; sprinkle with pepper. Chill. Cut bacon into small pieces and cook until crisp. Mix remaining ingredients, add bacon and pour over spinach. Toss until spinach is coated and slightly wilted. Serve on two salad plates.

*Tim Kuykendall
Springfield, IL*

Chinese Cabbage Salad with Chicken

A generous sprinkling of bright green cilantro adds snap to this new favorite.

1 small cabbage, shredded
1 bunch green onions, chopped, including tops
1 pkg. fresh mushrooms, chopped
3 or 4 skinned chicken breasts, cooked and chopped
½ cup oil
½ cup seasoned rice vinegar
1 tsp. sugar
1 tsp. salt
1 pkg. chicken-flavored ramen noodles

Combine cabbage, green onions, mushrooms and chopped chicken. In a separate bowl, mix oil, vinegar, sugar, salt and the seasoning packet from the ramen noodles. Pour dressing over cabbage mixture. Crumble ramen noodles onto a foil-lined cookie sheet and broil until brown. Spread the noodles evenly over the top of the salad.

Hint Cover uncooked chicken breasts with water in a microwave-safe bowl. Add garlic powder and cook in microwave.

You can also add walnuts, pecans or sesame seeds to the noodle topping.

*Jeanette Creamer
Jacksonville, FL*

Strawberry Spinach Salad

Try preparing this salad with baby spinach leaves and wild strawberries. The sweet and tender leaves and juicy berries are perfect complements.

Salad

½ to ¾ lb. fresh spinach,
   washed and dried
1 pint strawberries,
   hulled and sliced
2 oz. slivered almonds, toasted

Dressing

½ cup sugar
¼ cup cider vinegar
2 T. sesame seeds
1 T. poppy seeds
1 T. minced red onion
½ tsp. Worcestershire sauce
¼ tsp. paprika
½ cup vegetable oil

Arrange spinach and berries in a clear glass salad bowl. Place all dressing ingredients, except oil, in a blender. Blend well. With blender on low speed, slowly add oil in a steady stream until incorporated. Drizzle dressing over salad. Garnish with almonds.

Cynthia Cernauskas
Valparaiso, IN

Swedish Beet Salad with Horseradish Dressing

This salad goes great as a side dish to any meats or serve it warm with pork spare ribs rubbed with fresh sage and coriander seeds.

4 medium beets, about 1½ to 2 inches in diameter
2 tsp. distilled white vinegar
4 tsp. sugar
Salt
Pinch of ground cloves
2 tsp. vegetable oil
2 to 4 tsp. peeled, finely grated, fresh horseradish or 4 tsp. prepared hot
  white horseradish
1 to 2 tsp. chopped, fresh parsley

Rinse beets, taking care not to pierce skins. Put in saucepan, cover with water and bring to a boil. Cover and simmer over low heat 20 to 30 minutes or until tender. Let cool. Run beets under cold water and slip off the skins. Slice beets.

In a small bowl, whisk vinegar with sugar, salt, cloves and oil. Stir in horseradish. Put beets in shallow serving dish, pour dressing over beet slices, turning each over to coat well. Garnish with parsley. (Salad can be kept 2 days in the refrigerator if covered.) Makes 4 servings.

Sharon Walker
Medford, MN

Soups

Mushroom Soup

Serve this soup with crusty bread and wedges of your favorite cheeses.

1½ oz. dried chanterelle
   mushrooms
1½ oz. dried mushrooms, sliced
1 portobello mushroom
3 (14½-oz.) cans beef broth
3 onions, chopped
2 carrots, chopped
4 parsley roots, chopped
2 celery stalks, chopped
2 T. parsley, chopped
3 (10¾-oz.) cans cream of
   potato soup
2½ cups milk

Soak the dried mushrooms in a quart of warm water (or enough water to cover mushrooms) for 1 to 2 hours. Add beef broth and vegetables. Cook slowly for about an hour or until vegetables are tender. Add cream of potato soup and milk. Cook another 30 minutes and serve hot. Yields 12 servings.

*Suzanne M. Wynn
Cheektowaga, NY*

appetizers

relishes

salads

soups

breads

side
dishes

main
dishes

desserts

Winter Squash Soup

Cook the squash and carrots in water until they are tender,
or roast in a 375°F oven for 1 hour or until tender.

5 cups cubed, peeled winter
    squash
7 large carrots, sliced
16 oz. whole-milk ricotta
    cheese
1 small onion, finely chopped
1 egg, beaten
1 T. butter
2 T. chopped, fresh sage leaves
    or 1 T. crushed, dried sage
2 tsp. salt

Cook squash and carrots in water until tender.
Drain and cool. Process in blender with ricotta
cheese until smooth. Combine purée in
saucepan with remaining ingredients. Cook
over medium heat for 15 to 20 minutes or
until heated through.

Darlene Kaderli
Albany, WI

Brian's Buffalo Breath Chili

Make this chili with homemade salsa and a mixture of chilies from your garden.

3 lbs. beef sirloin tips, cut into small pieces
2 tsp. vegetable oil
1 small yellow onion, chopped
20 oz. beef broth
3½ T. cumin seeds
½ tsp. dried Mexican oregano leaves
6 cloves garlic, minced
2 T. Mojave Hot New Mexico chili powder
1 T. Mojave ground Chili de Arbol

16 oz. thick and chunky salsa (mild or hot)
1 dried New Mexico chili pepper, boiled and pureed
2 or more of each of your favorite fresh chilies
    (red, yellow and green; mild and hot), seeded
    and cut into strips
½ cup brown sugar
Juice from 1 lime
1 tsp. Buffalo Jalapeño Mexican Hot Sauce
Flour tortillas

In a large saucepan or Dutch oven, brown beef in oil over medium heat. Add onion and enough beef broth to cover meat. Bring to a boil and boil for 15 minutes. Add cumin and oregano. Reduce heat to a simmer, and add half of the garlic and half of the chili powders. Simmer for 15 minutes.

Transfer mixture to a slow cooker. Add salsa, New Mexico chili pepper, the hottest of the fresh-cut chilies, remaining garlic and remaining chili powders. Cook on High for 1 hour, stirring occasionally. (You can also simmer on the stove top over medium heat.) Add remaining fresh chilies. Simmer for 30 minutes longer, stirring occasionally.

Stir in brown sugar, lime juice and Jalapeño Hot Sauce. Simmer on low heat until ready to serve. Serve with warm flour tortillas.

Brian Lentz
Cotati, CA

White Chili

Freeze fresh-picked corn during the bountiful harvest and use it when making this recipe.

2 T. olive oil
1 large onion, chopped
1 rib celery, diced
1 cup sliced, fresh mushrooms
2 cloves garlic, minced
1 lb. ground turkey (or ground beef or protein vegetable substitute)
16-oz. can cannellini beans, rinsed and drained
11-oz. can white corn, rinsed and drained or 16 oz. yellow corn, thawed
4-oz. can chopped green chili peppers
1 tsp. ground cumin
1 tsp. ground oregano
½ tsp. Tabasco or other hot sauce
1 cup sour cream
Hot, cooked rice
1 cup shredded Monterey Jack cheese
2 T. snipped fresh cilantro

In a large saucepan, heat 1 tablespoon oil over medium heat. Add onion, celery, mushrooms and garlic. Sauté for 5 minutes. Remove vegetables from pan and set aside. Heat remaining tablespoon of oil in a pan over medium heat. Add turkey, breaking it apart with wooden spoon. Cook until no longer pink.

Return vegetables to pan along with beans, corn, chilies, cumin, oregano and hot sauce. Mix well and heat through. Stir in sour cream. Heat, but do not boil. Serve chili over rice and sprinkle with cheese and cilantro.

Viola Little
Huntington, NY

Beef and Vegetable Stew

Make this great stew with fresh vegetables from your garden. And save a few of these summer treasures in your freezer, to use in the cooler months.

3 qts. water
3 to 4 cups stewing beef, cut into
  cubes
6 potatoes, diced
1½ cups peas
1½ cups sliced carrots
1½ cups corn kernels
1½ cups cut green beans
8-oz. can tomato sauce

In a stock pot, combine water, beef and potatoes. Bring to a boil. Reduce heat and simmer until beef and potatoes are tender. Add remaining ingredients. Simmer for 10 to 15 minutes longer.

Lisa Carter
Fernandina Beach, FL

Southern Low Country Seafood Chowder

A sweet onion and gathering of fresh herbs season this seafood & corn chowder.

1 large Vidalia onion, finely diced
¼ cup unsalted butter
2 cups milk or half-and-half
1 cup corn kernels
1 T. cornstarch
2 cups fresh shrimp, peeled
2 cups fresh crabmeat, uncooked

Seasonings to taste:
Salt and pepper
Garlic
Chives
Parsley
Celery seed
Tabasco or other hot sauce
1 tsp. sorghum (optional)

In a soup pot, lightly sauté onion in butter over medium heat. Add seasonings to taste. Cook and stir for 3 minutes. Add milk, corn and cornstarch. Bring to a simmer. Add shrimp and crabmeat. Simmer for 10 minutes.

Hint Thin chowder with champagne, if necessary.

Barbara Harmon
Camden, SC

Carrot and Mushroom Soup

Slice a variety of available mushrooms for this soup.

¼ cup butter
1½ lbs. fresh mushrooms, sliced
2 cups thinly sliced carrots
½ cup chopped onions
3 to 4 cups chicken broth
¼ cup Madeira wine or dry sherry
1 to 2 T. finely chopped fresh dill
Salt and pepper to taste

In a large saucepan, melt butter over medium heat. Add mushrooms, carrots and onions. Sauté for 5 minutes. Add stock. Bring to a boil. Reduce heat, cover and simmer for 15 to 20 minutes or until carrots are tender. Add Madeira, dill, salt and pepper.

Sue Minter
South Range, WI

All-Day Stew

Bake this stew in the fall when you are working in the yard, raking leaves or preparing your garden for the winter months.

2 lbs. cubed beef round steak
6 potatoes, peeled and quartered
6 medium carrots, peeled and sliced
3 medium onions, coarsely chopped
2 (10¾-oz.) cans condensed tomato soup
1½ soup cans water
1 large bay leaf
1 tsp. salt
Pepper to taste
Dash Worcestershire sauce
16-oz. pkg. frozen or fresh peas

Heat oven to 250°F. Combine all ingredients, except peas, in a large casserole dish. Bake stew, covered, for 5 hours. Add peas during the last 15 minutes of cooking. Remove bay leaf before serving.

Hint You can also cook this at 275°F for 4 hours.

Rose Boyer
Hecker, IL

Jim's Potato Soup

Complement this creamy soup with fresh watercress salad.

⅓ cup diced celery
⅓ cup diced carrot
¼ cup diced onion
1 clove garlic, minced
3 T. butter
5 T. flour
1 qt. milk
3 chicken bouillon cubes
2 T. fresh parsley
½ tsp. salt
½ tsp. seasoned salt
1 T. fresh chives
¼ tsp. cayenne pepper
6 medium potatoes, cooked, cooled, peeled and chopped
¼ lb. bacon, cooked and crumbled
Shredded cheddar cheese

In a large saucepan, sauté celery, carrot, onion and garlic in butter. Stir in flour. Gradually add milk. Cook until thick. Add remaining ingredients except potatoes, bacon bits and cheese. Simmer for 20 minutes. Add potatoes and simmer for 20 to 25 minutes more. Garnish with crumbled bacon and shredded cheese.

Marcella West (Moore)
Washington, IL

Spicy Chili

Make your favorite cornbread, adding young sweet corn cut from the cob into the batter to accompany this wonderful chili. Use tomatoes from your pantry for the chili recipe.

8 slices thick-sliced bacon
8 oz. mild Italian sausage (use medium or hot for spicier chili)
1½ lbs. stew meat, cut into ½ inch cubes
2 large onions, chopped
2 large green peppers, chopped
3 cloves garlic, crushed
2 dried red chili peppers, crumbled
2 fresh jalapeño peppers, seeded and chopped
1½ T. chili powder
½ tsp. salt
1 tsp. ground cumin
1 tsp. dried oregano leaves
2 tsp. sugar
14-oz. can whole tomatoes, undrained and chopped
12-oz. can tomato paste
12-oz. can beer
16-oz. can pinto beans, drained

Cook bacon until crisp in a large Dutch oven; drain and crumble. Set aside. Drain all but 2 tablespoons of drippings from the pan. Brown sausage in bacon drippings; transfer to paper towels to drain. Slice sausage and set aside. Drain all but 2 tablespoons of drippings from Dutch oven. Add beef, onion, green pepper and garlic to drippings in Dutch oven. Sauté until beef is browned. Add all ingredients except the pinto beans. Bring to a boil, cover, reduce heat and simmer for 1½ hours, stirring occasionally. Stir in beans and simmer uncovered for 30 minutes more. Yields 8 servings.

Janice M. Boller
Minneapolis, MN

South of the Border Chicken Soup

This soup is delicious made with garden peas, carrots, corn or beans. Simply substitute 2 cups of these vegetables for the can of mixed vegetables.

2 T. vegetable oil
3 corn tortillas, cut into ½-inch strips
⅔ cup chopped green bell pepper
⅓ cup chopped onion
1 clove garlic, minced
¼ cup all-purpose flour
2 (12-oz.) cans chicken broth
2 cups cubed, cooked chicken
15-oz. can mixed vegetables, undrained
1 tsp. chili powder

Heat oil in a deep skillet. Add tortilla strips and fry, stirring constantly, until golden. Drain on paper-towel-lined plate. Add pepper and onion to skillet. Sauté until tender. Add garlic, then stir in flour. Gradually stir in chicken broth. Stir in remaining ingredients and cook until heated through.

Mrs. David Ross
Henderson, TN

Zucchini-Tortellini Soup

Pick zucchini, spinach and basil from the garden and add to this soup.

2 T. butter or olive oil
5 cloves garlic, minced
2 (14½-oz.) cans chicken broth
½ to 1 lb. zucchini, cut into 1-inch chunks
9-oz. pkg. fresh cheese tortellini
½ cup grated Parmesan cheese
14½-oz. can stewed tomatoes
½ cup spinach, stemmed
6 fresh basil leaves, chopped (or 1 tsp. dried basil
    leaves)
¼ cup chopped, fresh parsley
Salt and pepper to taste

In a large saucepan, sauté garlic in butter for 2 minutes. Stir in broth, zucchini and tortellini. Bring to a boil and reduce heat. Stir in Parmesan cheese. Simmer for 5 minutes or until tortellini and zucchini are tender. Stir in tomatoes, spinach, basil and parsley. Simmer for 2 minutes. Add salt and pepper to taste. Serve garnished with additional Parmesan cheese.

Cecilia Martinez
San Fernando, CA

New Orleans Sweet Potato Chowder

This chowder is made from leftover sweet potatoes and green vegetables, so there is no need of lengthy cooking to develop the rich flavors.

1 cup finely diced celery
1 cup finely diced onion
1 cup grated carrots
1 cup finely diced green and/or red bell pepper
2 T. vegetable oil
2 qts. turkey stock or chicken broth
Leftover, mashed sweet potatoes or turnips
2 cups diced, cooked turkey
2 cups diced ham
Leftover green vegetables (lima beans, string beans, spinach, etc.)
Handful of fresh parsley, finely chopped
1 T. cayenne pepper
1 T. paprika
Salt and pepper to taste

In a stock pot, sauté celery, onion, carrots and bell pepper in oil until vegetables are tender. Add stock and bring to a simmer. Add remaining ingredients and return to a simmer. Simmer until heated through.

Irene Smith
New York, NY

Cauliflower Soup

Chop some extra parsley for serving at the table.

2 T. butter or margarine
½ cup onion, chopped
1 cup celery, thinly sliced
2 small carrots, grated
3 medium potatoes, peeled and thinly sliced
1 large head cauliflower, cut into florets
4 cups chicken broth
¼ cup butter or margarine
¼ cup flour
2 cups milk
Salt and pepper to taste
Parsley
1 cup half-and-half
8 oz. shredded sharp cheddar cheese

Heat 2 tablespoons butter or margarine in a large pan over medium heat. Add onion and sauté until transparent. Add celery, carrots, potatoes, cauliflower and chicken broth. Cover and simmer for 15 to 20 minutes.

In a 2-quart saucepan, make white sauce by mixing ¼ cup butter, flour and milk. When thick, add salt, pepper, parsley and half-and-half. Pour mixture into soup. Blend well. Simmer 15 to 20 minutes. Sprinkle cheese on top of individual soup bowls. Yields 10 servings.

Jayne Eiben
Shell Rock, IA

Vegtaburger Soup

Let this soup simmer while you work in your garden.

Water
½ lb. ground meat (of your choice)
5 medium potatoes, cubed
3 fresh carrots, sliced
2 cups fresh corn kernels
¼ lb. fresh string beans
7 plum tomatoes, chopped
½ head cabbage, sliced
15-oz. can crushed tomatoes
8-oz. can tomato sauce
1 cube beef bouillon
1 clove garlic, crushed
1 T. chopped, fresh basil leaves or 1
    tsp. dried basil leaves
1 T. chopped, fresh parsley or 1 tsp.
    dried parsley flakes
1 tsp. salt
2 whole bay leaves
2 tsp. chopped, fresh oregano or ½
    tsp. dried oregano leaves
¼ tsp. pepper

Fill a large soup pot half full of water. Add ground meat and bring to a boil. Add vegetables and simmer until vegetables are almost tender. Add remaining ingredients. Simmer until vegetables are tender. Serve hot.

Note You can substitute fresh spinach for cabbage.

Lynda Gosson
Philadelphia, PA

Cabbage Soup

Serve this soup with sour cream and a sprig of thyme garnish.

4 strips bacon
4 cups shredded cabbage
2 medium onions, sliced
1 tsp. caraway seeds
6 cups chicken broth (or enough to cover vegetables)
½ cup vermouth
Salt and freshly cracked pepper to taste
Sour cream

In heavy pot, cook bacon until crisp. Remove from pot and crumble; set aside. Add cabbage, onions and caraway seeds to bacon drippings. Cook and stir until cabbage is just barely tender, about 10 minutes. Add chicken broth and vermouth. Bring to a boil. Cover. Reduce heat and simmer for 25 minutes. Add bacon, salt and pepper. Serve garnished with a dollop of sour cream.

Sue Minter
South Range, WI

Chapter 5

Breads

Smith Creek Huckleberry Bread

Huckleberries are wild, blue-black berries that closely resemble blueberries. It is unlikely to find fresh huckleberries at the market, so you'll have to pick them yourself. Substitute blueberries, blackberries or even raspberries if there aren't any huckleberry bushes around.

1½ cups sugar
½ cup vegetable shortening
2 eggs
1 tsp. vanilla
3 cups all-purpose flour
1 cup milk
1 T. baking powder
1 tsp. salt
2 cups fresh huckleberries

Heat oven to 350°F. Blend sugar, shortening, eggs and vanilla with electric mixer. Add remaining ingredients, except huckleberries. Mix well. Fold in huckleberries. Pour batter into two 5 x 7-inch greased loaf pans. Bake for 55 minutes.

Alisa Conger
Chattaroy, WA

appetizers

relishes

salads

soups

breads

side
dishes

main
dishes

desserts

Cranberry-Nut Bread

Make loaves of this bread and give as gifts with citrus fruits such as grapefruit and oranges.

Bread
1 cup sugar
¾ cup water
½ cup orange juice
2 T. vegetable oil
1 egg
1 T. grated orange peel
2 cups all-purpose flour
1½ tsp. baking powder
1 tsp. salt
½ tsp. baking soda
1 cup halved, fresh cranberries
1 cup chopped nuts

Glaze
2 cups powdered sugar
2 T. butter, softened
3 to 4 T. milk
½ tsp. vanilla

Heat oven to 350°F. Grease a 9 x 5-inch loaf pan. In large bowl, combine sugar, water, orange juice, oil, egg and orange peel. Mix well. Add flour, baking powder, salt and baking soda. Stir until moistened. Stir in cranberries and nuts. Pour into prepared pan.

Bake for 50 to 60 minutes or until toothpick inserted in center comes out clean. Cool for 10 minutes, then remove from pan. When loaf is completely cool, combine glaze ingredients. Microwave glaze on high for 30 seconds, stir and drizzle over loaf.

Eva Keith
Mt. Juliet, TN

Swedish Cardamom Eggnog Wreath

This is also a delicious bread to give as a gift. Bread can be baked ahead and frozen; decorate with icing before presenting to the lucky recipient.

Bread
1 pkg. active dry yeast
¼ cup warm water (105°F to 115°F)
1¼ cups eggnog
½ cup sugar
6 T. butter
1 egg yolk
¾ tsp. ground cardamom
¼ tsp. salt
3½ to 4 cups all-purpose flour
Candied cherries

Icing
1 cup powdered sugar
2 T. eggnog
1 tsp. rum flavoring
⅛ tsp. ground nutmeg

In large bowl, dissolve yeast in warm water. Let stand for 5 minutes. Combine with eggnog, sugar, butter, egg yolk, cardamom and salt. Stir in enough flour to form a dough that pulls away from sides of bowl. Turn dough onto lightly floured surface. Knead for 5 minutes or until dough is smooth and elastic.

Place dough in greased bowl, turning to coat dough. Cover and let rise in warm place until dough is doubled in size (about 2 hours). Divide dough into 3 equal portions. Roll each portion into a 24-inch rope. Loosely braid ropes, pinching ends together. Place on baking sheet, curving into wreath shape. Let rise in warm place until doubled in size (about 1 hour).

Heat oven to 325°F. Bake wreath for 40 minutes or until browned. Cool for 20 minutes. Combine icing ingredients, stirring until smooth. Drizzle icing over wreath. Decorate wreath with cherries.

Mary Jane Smith
Brigham City, UT

Sesame Soup Crackers

Try making these crackers with different blends of seeds: mixtures of sesame and poppy; or sesame, mustard and celery seeds. Serve these crackers with cheese, cucumbers, radishes and sunflower sprouts.

½ cup water
6 T. vegetable oil
½ tsp. salt
2 cups whole wheat flour
½ cup sesame seeds + ¼ cup sesame seeds
Salt (to sprinkle on dough)

Heat oven to 350°F and grease large cookie sheet. Blend the first three ingredients with electric mixer. Add flour and ¼ cup sesame seeds and mix well. Knead for 1 minute and let dough rest for 10 minutes. Roll out dough thinly and place on cookie sheet. Sprinkle with more sesame seeds and a little salt. Use the rolling pin to roll over the sheet of dough once again so the seeds will stick to the dough. Prick dough with fork. Bake for 15 minutes. Cut into crackers while still warm.

Martha Farmwald
Nappanee, IN

Cherry-Nut Bread

Try substituting tart cherries, picked off the tree, in place of the maraschino cherries.

8-oz. pkg. cream cheese, softened
1½ cups sugar
1 cup butter or margarine, softened
1½ tsp. vanilla
4 eggs

2¼ cups sifted cake flour, divided
1¼ tsp. baking powder
¾ cup chopped maraschino cherries
½ cup chopped nuts or miniature
    chocolate chips

Heat oven to 325°F. Combine cheese, sugar, butter and vanilla until smooth. Add eggs, one at a time, beating well after each addition. Gradually add 2 cups flour and the baking powder. Toss remaining ¼ cup flour with cherries and nuts. Fold mixture into batter.

Divide batter evenly among 3 greased coffee cans. Bake for 1 hour or until tops are golden brown and a toothpick inserted in center comes out clean. Cool completely. To remove bread from cans, open sealed end of cans and gently push out bread.

Note This recipe cannot be doubled. The bread won't rise.

Regina Gambino
Hamburg, NY

Hobo Bread

Add variety to this bread by substituting dried cherries, cranberries or chopped apricots for the raisins.

2 cups raisins
2 cups boiling water
2 T. margarine
2 tsp. baking soda
2 eggs
4 cups all-purpose flour
2 cups sugar
½ cup chopped nuts
1 tsp. ground cinnamon
½ tsp. salt

Heat oven to 350°F. Combine the raisins, water, margarine and baking soda. Let cool. Add eggs; mix well. Stir in remaining ingredients. Grease and flour three 1-pound coffee cans. Fill each half full. Bake for 1 hour. Let bread cool completely in cans. Remove round loaves from cans and slice.

Ophelia Wade
Kennett, MO

Boston Brown Bread

Stack this bread with garden lettuce and marinated vegetables for a great sandwich.

1 cup sugar
½ cup vegetable oil
½ cup molasses
2 eggs, beaten
2 cups all-purpose flour
2 tsp. baking soda
1 tsp. salt
1 cup boiling water

Heat oven to 350°F. Spray a 9 x 5-inch loaf pan with nonstick cooking spray. With electric mixer, cream together sugar, oil, molasses and eggs on medium speed. In a separate bowl, combine flour, baking soda and salt. Gradually beat flour mixture into egg mixture. Mix well.

Reduce mixer speed to low and add boiling water. Pour batter into prepared pan. Bake for 45 to 50 minutes or until toothpick inserted in center of loaf comes out clean. Cool bread in pan for 10 minutes, then turn out on cooling rack to cool.

Eva Keith
Mt. Juliet, TN

Crusty Cloverleaf Rolls

Try adding a mixture of ¼ cup of your favorite blend of garden herbs with the flour, to make these delightful rolls into herb rolls.

2 cups warm water (105°F)
2 T. active dry yeast
½ cup sugar
2 eggs (room temperature)
¼ cup vegetable oil
1 T. salt
6 to 6½ cups all-purpose flour
Butter

In large bowl, dissolve yeast in water. Stir in sugar, eggs, oil and salt. Add 3 cups flour. Beat until smooth. Mix in enough remaining flour to make a dough that is easy to handle. Turn dough onto lightly floured surface. Knead until smooth and elastic (8 to 10 minutes), adding flour as necessary to prevent sticking. Place dough in greased bowl, turning to coat dough. Cover and let rise in warm place until double, about 1 hour.

Punch down dough. Grease hands and muffin tins. Pinch a 1-inch ball of dough, turning edges under to middle to form a smooth ball. Place three balls in each cup of a muffin tin. Cover and let rise until double, about 1 hour.

Heat oven to 350°F. Bake rolls until dark golden brown and they sound hollow when tapped with fingernail. Brush tops with butter and place on cooling rack.

Doris Bjork
Lawton, OK

breads

69

Banana Bread

If you have any left (and that's a big "if"),
make French toast with this bread. Top it with
a sprinkling of powdered sugar.

1³/₄ cups all-purpose flour
2 tsp. baking powder
½ tsp. baking soda
½ tsp. ground cinnamon
½ tsp. ground nutmeg
½ tsp. salt
2 ripe bananas, mashed
¾ cup sugar
2 eggs
¼ cup butter, melted
¼ cup milk
1 cup chopped nuts
1 6-oz. pkg. butterscotch chips

Heat oven to 350°F. Sift together flour, baking powder, baking soda, cinnamon, nutmeg and salt. Set aside. Combine bananas, sugar, eggs and melted butter. Blend well. Alternately stir in flour mixture and milk. Stir in nuts and butterscotch chips. Pour batter into a greased 9 x 5-inch loaf pan or two small loaf pans. Bake for 50 minutes to 1 hour or until toothpick inserted in center comes out clean. (Small loaves will take less time.)

Treva Woodard
West Palm Beach, FL

Lefse

Lefse is a traditional Scandinavian flatbread. It is delicious served with fruit and berry preserves or jam.

6 cups riced, cooked potatoes, cooled
1½ cups all-purpose flour
2 T. butter, softened
2 tsp. salt
2 tsp. sugar

Combine all ingredients. Use more or less flour as necessary to make a dough that can be formed into balls and rolled out. (This will depend on the moisture of the potatoes.) Roll out balls of dough very thin on floured pastry cloth. The size of the rolled out dough will depend on the size of your griddle.

Cook lefse on hot griddle until brown spots appear on bottom. Turn lefse and cook other side. To serve lefse, smear butter on it and sprinkle with sugar, then roll it up.

Lois Christiansen
Hartland, MN

Easy Beer Bread

Make hearty sandwiches with this wonderful, easy bread. Try filling them with sliced tomatoes, cucumber and sprouts.

3 cups self-rising flour
1 12-oz. can warm beer
2 T. sugar

Heat oven to 375°F. Combine all ingredients and mix well. Pour batter into 2 greased and floured loaf pans. Bake for 45 minutes.

Katie Ruimerman
Middletown, CT

Zucchini Muffins

Blend a sprinkling of nutmeg and cloves into softened butter; serve this butter with these delicious muffins.

1⅓ cups sugar
3 eggs
½ cup vegetable oil
½ cup orange juice
1 tsp. almond extract
2½ cups all-purpose flour
2 tsp. ground cinnamon
2 tsp. baking powder
1 tsp. baking soda
1 tsp. salt
½ tsp. ground cloves
1½ cups shredded zucchini

Heat oven to 350°F. In a mixing bowl, beat sugar, eggs, oil, orange juice and almond extract until smooth. In a separate bowl, combine flour, cinnamon, baking powder, baking soda, salt and cloves. Add to the egg mixture. Mix well. Stir in zucchini. Fill greased muffin cups two-thirds full with batter. Bake for 20 to 25 minutes or until browned.

Harriet Link
Renville, MN

Favorite Bran Muffins

Fruit or berry jam bakes inside bran muffins.

4 cups All Bran cereal
1 cup hot water
5 cups all-purpose flour
5 tsp. baking soda
4 eggs
1 lb. brown sugar
1 qt. buttermilk
2 cups quick-cooking rolled oats
1 cup olive oil or canola oil
Favorite jam

Heat oven to 350°F. Combine cereal and hot water in a large bowl. Cover and set aside. Sift flour and baking soda together. Beat the eggs well. Add sugar, buttermilk, oats and oil. Mix well. Stir in flour mixture. Fold in bran cereal, mixing well.

Fill paper-lined muffin tins two-thirds full with batter. Top with 1 teaspoon jam, then additional batter to cover. Bake for 25 to 30 minutes.

Hint Substitute nuts, fresh berries or raisins for jam.

Lillian Zemmin
Grosse Pte. Woods, MI

Zucchini-Nut Loaf

Make this quick nut bread with zucchini or yellow squash in the summer. In the fall try substituting winter squash or sweet potatoes.

1 cup shredded zucchini
1 cup sugar
1 egg
½ cup vegetable oil
1½ cups all-purpose flour
1 tsp. ground cinnamon
½ tsp. baking soda
½ tsp. ground nutmeg
½ tsp. salt
¼ tsp. baking powder
¼ tsp. finely shredded lemon peel (or lemon juice)
½ cup chopped walnuts

Heat oven to 325°F. In mixing bowl, beat together zucchini, sugar and egg. Add oil and mix well. In a second bowl, combine flour, cinnamon, baking soda, nutmeg, salt, baking powder and lemon peel. (If using lemon juice, add it to zucchini mixture.) Stir flour mixture into zucchini mixture. Fold in nuts.

Pour batter into a greased loaf pan. Bake for 60 to 65 minutes or until toothpick inserted in center comes out clean. Cool in pan on cooling rack. Remove loaf from pan. Wrap and store overnight before slicing.

Alice Kingsley
Aurora, IL

Orange Dinner Rolls

Delicious, homemade citrus rolls get their flavor from orange juice concentrate and grated orange peel. Create variations of these rolls by substituting lemonade concentrate or fruit juices of blood orange, mango or carrots.

¾ cup milk
⅓ cup butter or margarine
¼ cup water
2 pkgs. active dry yeast or rapid-rise yeast
⅓ cup sugar
1 tsp. salt
4½ cups all-purpose flour
2 eggs
¼ cup orange juice concentrate
½ cup grated orange with peel, divided
Melted butter

Heat milk, butter and water in microwave or on stove top until warm and butter is partially melted. In a large bowl, mixer or bread machine, combine, in order, yeast, sugar, salt, flour, eggs, orange juice concentrate, ¼ cup grated orange with peel, and milk mixture. Stir until dough forms. Knead for 5 minutes. Put dough in a greased bowl, turning to coat dough. Cover with plastic wrap. Let rise in warm place for 1¼ hours (rapid-rise yeast will rise sooner), or refrigerate dough for 2 hours (up to 2 days).

Punch dough down when risen. Roll dough into a large rectangle. Spread remaining ¼ cup grated orange with peel over rectangle. Starting from long edge, roll up dough. Cut in 1-inch slices and place in greased muffin cups. Cover and let rise again for 30 to 45 minutes.

Heat oven to 325°F. Bake rolls for 15 to 20 minutes. Don't let tops brown. Brush tops of rolls with melted butter. Serve warm.

Kristine Brunkhorst
Waverly, IA

Chocolate Zucchini Bread

Serve this bread with butter or cream cheese you have blended with marmalade.

3 eggs
1 cup oil
2 cups sugar
1 T. vanilla
2 cups zucchini, peeled and
    shredded
2½ cups flour
½ cup baking cocoa
1 tsp. salt
1 tsp. baking soda
1 tsp. cinnamon
¼ tsp. baking powder

Heat oven to 350°F. In mixing bowl, beat eggs, oil, sugar and vanilla. Stir in zucchini. Combine dry ingredients. Add to zucchini mixture and mix well. Pour into two 8 x 4 x 2-inch loaf pans. Bake for 1 hour or until bread tests done. Yields two loaves.

Judy Alvard
Hudsonville, MI

6
Chapter

Side Dishes

Grilled Vegetables

Sample an herb blend of 2 tablespoons fresh basil, rosemary and oregano sprinkled on these grilled vegetables.

¼ cup olive oil
1 T. lemon juice
2 tsp. minced garlic
2 T. chopped, fresh oregano or 2 tsp. dried oregano leaves
1 lb. assorted vegetables (eggplant, summer squash, bell peppers,
    mushrooms, onions or small red potatoes)

Combine oil, lemon juice, garlic and oregano. Set marinade aside. Cut all vegetables, except onions, into bite-sized pieces. Cut onions into wedges.

Place vegetable pieces and marinade in a sealable plastic bag. Refrigerate for several hours, turning every 30 minutes. Grill vegetables for 10 to 20 minutes or until tender, basting with any remaining marinade as needed.

Jo-Ann and Jim Maxwell
Bay City, MI

appetizers

relishes

salads

soups

breads

side
dishes

main
dishes

desserts

Harvard Beets

Beets are garden staples; some unique varieties to plant are chioggia striped beets with their bright candy-red exteriors, and the golden beet, which is golden-orange throughout.

2 to 3 cups sliced, peeled beets
½ cup water
2 T. butter or margarine
1 T. sugar
1 T. cornstarch
¼ tsp. salt

Heat oven to 350°F. Place beets in casserole dish. Combine water, butter, sugar, cornstarch and salt in a saucepan. Stir and cook over medium heat until mixture thickens. Pour over beets, stirring to coat. Cover and bake for 1 hour or until beets are tender.

Karen Grimm
Cologne, MN

Pilaf-Style Orzo

Grilled onions, eggplant and zucchini served with crusty bread make a great menu for this recipe.

¾ cup chopped onion
1 clove garlic, minced
2 T. olive oil
1½ cups uncooked orzo pasta (rosamarina)
3 cups chicken broth (or as much as is needed)
Salt and pepper to taste
2 T. finely chopped fresh parsley

In a large skillet, sauté onion and garlic in oil just until tender. Add the orzo and stir until coated with oil. Add the broth and stir to moisten the orzo. Season with salt and pepper. Simmer until all the broth is absorbed, about 15 minutes. Add the parsley and toss to combine.

Hint Recipe can easily be doubled.

Virginia Sendek
Huntington, WV

Cabbage Casserole

Serve this casserole with grilled pork chops for a hearty supper.

4 cups crushed cornflakes
¾ cup butter, melted
4 cups shredded cabbage
10¾-oz. can cream of celery soup
1 cup whole milk
½ cup mayonnaise
½ cup chopped onion
¼ tsp. salt
¼ tsp. pepper
2 cups shredded mild cheddar cheese

Heat oven to 375°F. Mix cornflakes and butter together. Pat half in bottom of an 8 x 12-inch (2-quart) casserole dish. Spread cabbage over cornflakes.

Combine soup, milk, mayonnaise, onion, salt and pepper. Pour over cabbage. Spread cheese over top of mixture. Sprinkle remaining cornflake mixture over cheese. Bake for 25 minutes or until golden brown and bubbly around edges.

Cynthia Hoffman
Bessemer City, NC

Vegetable Ratatouille

For a rustic alternative, cut the vegetables into chunks, wedges or strips.

4 T. vegetable oil or olive oil
1 medium eggplant, cut into thin small pieces
2 large onions, chopped
4 cloves garlic, finely chopped
1 green bell pepper, seeded and chopped

1 red bell pepper, seeded and chopped
2 thin zucchini, cut into thin rounds
2 large tomatoes, cut into small pieces
½ cup chopped, fresh basil leaves, divided
Salt and pepper to taste

Heat oil in a large skillet. Sauté eggplant for 5 minutes until lightly browned, turning often. Add onions, garlic and peppers. Sauté for 5 more minutes. Add zucchini, tomatoes and half of the basil leaves. Cover and simmer over low heat for 20 minutes. Remove the lid and cook until all the liquid evaporates, stirring occasionally. Season with salt and pepper. Chill overnight and garnish with remaining fresh basil. Serve cold or reheated. It can be served immediately after preparing, but the flavors blend better if allowed to sit until next day.

John Allen
Tuckerton, NJ

Carrot Casserole

Carrots and onions bake in a creamy cheddar cheese sauce.

4 cups sliced carrots
1 medium onion, chopped
1 T. butter or margarine
10¾-oz. can cream of celery soup (or other
    creamed soup)
½ to ¾ cup shredded cheddar cheese
Salt and pepper to taste
Stuffing mix

Heat oven to 350°F. Cook carrots in boiling water until tender. Drain. Sauté onion in butter until tender. Stir in soup, cheese, salt and pepper. Stir in carrots. Put mixture into a 2-quart casserole dish. Sprinkle with stuffing mix. Bake for 20 minutes or until hot and bubbly.

Bonnie Skidmore
Middlebury, VT

Frozen Corn

There are many flavorful varieties of sweet corn available. A few varieties to plant include the Double Gem, a white and yellow kernel; Early Sunglow, an early yellow corn; and Sugar Snow Corn, a sweet white corn.

8 cups corn kernels, cut off
   uncooked cobs
1½ cups water
½ cup butter
2 tsp. salt
1½ tsp. sugar

Combine all ingredients in a large kettle. Bring to a boil and cook for 5 minutes. Cool. Put corn in containers and freeze.

Note This is the only way I prepare corn for the freezer. You can enjoy fresh, right-from-the-cob corn all year.

Elizabeth Everitt
Lake Elmo, MN

Onion Stuffing

Prepare this stuffing with sweet, juicy varieties of onions. These varieties include Walla Walla, Vidalia and the Maui onion. Try sautéing the onions with a blend of ¼ cup thyme, sage and rosemary.

6 large onions, sliced into rings
Butter
2 slices toast, made into crumbs
Salt and pepper to taste
1 egg, beaten

Sauté onion rings in butter until tender. Add crumbs, salt and pepper. Cool, then add egg. Use mixture to stuff turkey or other bird.

Al Huelsman
Wichita, KS

Unique Baked Potatoes

These baked potatoes make a simple supper; just serve with a garden salad.

10 medium to large russet
   baking potatoes, scrubbed
Vegetable oil
2 large onions, chopped
1 small jar prepared yellow
   mustard
1 small jar horseradish (hot or
   mild)
6 T. margarine or butter
2 T. milk
2 tsp. salt
16 oz. cheddar cheese (mild,
   medium or sharp), sliced

Heat oven to 450°F. Generously grease potatoes with oil. Bake on baking sheet until tender when pierced with a fork. Cool slightly, then cut in half lengthwise. Scoop out pulp from skins and place pulp in a large bowl. Set skins aside.

With electric mixer, mash potato pulp. Add onions, mustard, horseradish, margarine, milk and salt. Mix well. Stuff potato skins with mixture. Place stuffed potatoes on baking sheet and bake for 15 minutes. Remove from oven and cover potatoes with thick slices of cheese. Return to oven and bake until cheese is melted.

Hint Potatoes can be baked in advance. Reheat potato pulp in the microwave before mixing.

Eva Keith
Mt. Juliet, TN

side
dishes

83

Tagliatelle with Butter and Sage

Adorning the plate with variegated sage in creamy white and green provides interest to the soft colors of the dish.

1 lb. tagliatelle
½ cup unsalted butter
   (or extra-virgin olive oil)
20 fresh sage leaves
¾ cup grated Parmesan cheese
Dash of salt

In large pot, bring 5 quarts of water to a boil. Meanwhile, in small saucepan melt butter over medium heat. Add sage and cook over low heat until butter starts to turn golden and sage darkens, about 5 minutes. Add tagliatelle to the boiling water for about 2 minutes, until they rise to the surface. Drain pasta and arrange on a warm platter. Pour sage-butter mixture over the top. Sprinkle with half the Parmesan cheese, salt to taste, and toss lightly. Sprinkle with remaining cheese. Serve immediately. Yields 6 servings.

Note This recipe may be used either as a side dish or a main course. Serve with garlic bread and a dry red wine.

Tim Kuykendall
Springfield, IL

Quick Corn-Chili Casserole

Serve this casserole with a salad of avocado, tomatoes and onion.

2 cans cream-style corn
¾ cup white or yellow cornmeal
4 eggs, beaten
¼ cup vegetable oil
2 cloves garlic, minced
2 to 3 yellow chilies or jalapeño peppers, seeded and chopped
2 cups shredded sharp cheddar cheese

Heat oven to 350°F. Mix together corn, cornmeal, eggs, oil and garlic. Pour half of mixture into a casserole dish that has been sprayed with nonstick cooking spray. Spread chilies, then cheese over the mixture. Pour the rest of the mixture over the cheese. Bake for approximately 1 hour, until firm and lightly browned.

Renita Debes
Wichita, KS

Zucchini Rounds

These zucchini pancakes are great on their own. They're also delicious stacked together with cream cheese, goat cheese or an herbed soft cheese.

$1/3$ cup biscuit mix
$1/4$ cup grated Parmesan cheese
$1/8$ tsp. pepper
2 eggs, slightly beaten
2 cups shredded, unpeeled zucchini
2 T. butter or margarine

Combine biscuit mix, Parmesan cheese and pepper. Stir in eggs just until moistened. Fold in zucchini. Shape mixture into 12 rounds (patties), using about 2 tablespoons mixture for each. In skillet, melt butter over medium heat. Cook rounds in skillet for 2 to 3 minutes per side or until browned.

Ann Hopp
Highland, KS

Garden Casserole

This is a simple and delicious way to prepare garden vegetables. Try making this recipe with fresh grated Parmesan cheese.

2 medium zucchini, cut into $1/4$-inch slices
1 medium yellow summer squash, cut into $1/4$-inch slices
1 medium tomato, cut into $1/4$-inch slices
1 medium onion, sliced and separated into rings
1 T. grated Parmesan cheese
1 T. chopped, fresh basil or $1/2$ tsp. dried basil leaves
Salt and pepper to taste

Heat oven to 350°F. In a $1\,1/2$-quart casserole dish, arrange zucchini and summer squash slices. (You'll need to overlap them.) Top with tomato slices, then onion rings. Sprinkle with remaining ingredients. Bake for 25 to 30 minutes or until vegetables are tender.

Nora LaRiviere
Springfield, MA

Creole-Style Okra

Although available fresh almost year-round in the South, the okra season for the rest of the country is from about May through October.

2 T. lard
1 lb. fresh okra, diced
1 onion, minced
1 cup diced potatoes
1 green bell pepper, seeded and
 minced
1 cup water
3 T. tomato paste
1 T. minced fresh parsley
1 clove garlic, minced

Melt lard in skillet over medium-high heat. Add remaining ingredients. Cook for 15 minutes, stirring occasionally, or until vegetables are tender.

Lenora Jackson
Sand Springs, OK

'Bhagare Baingan' Spicy Eggplant

A variation is to serve the eggplant with wedges of garden-ripe tomatoes drizzled with oil and vinegar.

2 medium eggplants, sliced
1 inch piece of ginger
6 cloves of garlic
1 tsp. cumin seeds
2 tsp. coriander powder
1/2 tsp. chili powder
1/2 tsp. turmeric

1 tsp. salt or lemon pepper
3 onions, sliced thin
1/2 lb. tomatoes
1/4 cup oil
Green hot chilies, to taste
1/4 cup vinegar
1/2 cup brown sugar

Slice the eggplants with the skins, and place the slices in a pan of water with a pinch of salt. Grind the ginger and garlic to a grainy paste. Mix together all the dry spices. Slice the onions and cut the tomatoes into salad-type slices.

Heat oil in deep skillet. Brown the onions, garlic and ginger. Add the dry spices and stir. Add the tomatoes and chilies and cover for 5 minutes. Add the eggplant, stir and cover again, cooking the mixture on low heat for 6 to 7 minutes. When the eggplant is soft, stir in the vinegar, and then add the brown sugar. Cook for 1 minute. Serve hot with rice or pita bread.

Grace Phillips
Danbury, CT

Famous Chapman Parsley Bread Stuffing

This stuffing is delicious made with dry bread crumbs from homemade bread.

½ cup butter
1 cup chopped celery
½ cup chopped onion
3 qts. dry bread crumbs
2 cups chopped, fresh parsley
1 tsp. salt
1 T. chopped, fresh thyme leaves or 1 tsp. dried
   thyme leaves
½ tsp. pepper
2 eggs, beaten

Heat oven to 350°F. Melt butter in skillet over medium heat. Add celery and onion, and sauté until tender. In a large bowl, combine celery, onion, bread crumbs, parsley, salt, thyme and pepper. Add eggs and mix well. Spoon mixture into baking pan. Bake for 30 minutes or until heated through.

Note Use this mixture to stuff a turkey or chicken.

Linda Chapman
Spencer, IN

Ernest's Killer Potatoes

Prepare these scalloped potatoes with grated fresh Parmesan cheese.

5 medium potatoes, peeled and cubed
1 cup milk
½ tsp. salt
Pepper to taste
½ cup grated Parmesan cheese
1 T. paprika
½ cup butter, melted

Heat oven to 350°F. Spray a 9 x 13-inch baking dish with nonstick cooking spray. Place potatoes in baking dish in a single layer. Mix in milk, salt and pepper. Sprinkle with Parmesan cheese and paprika. Drizzle butter over all. Bake for 45 minutes to 1 hour or until potatoes are tender.

Note The trick is to only have one layer of potatoes, so they all get coated.

Kim Malone
Lakehills, TX

Sweet Potatoes in Orange Cups

A delicious, rich flavor is provided by red garnet or jewel sweet potatoes. Pipe the mashed sweet potatoes into orange halves and garnish with flowering thyme leaves.

4 sweet potatoes
2 oranges
2 T. butter
Ground nutmeg (optional)

Heat oven to 400°F. Peel, cook and mash sweet potatoes. Cut oranges in half and squeeze juice from oranges. Turn orange halves inside out and clean out pulp. Turn peels back for stuffing. Combine hot mashed potatoes, orange juice and butter. Fill orange cups with this mixture and sprinkle with nutmeg. Bake for 15 minutes or until heated through.

Kathy Niver
Hebron, CT

Scalloped Tomatoes

Fresh basil and thyme leaves with additional tomato slices make a beautiful garnish.

4 medium to large tomatoes
1 cup fresh bread crumbs
1/4 cup chopped, fresh parsley
2 T. minced green onions
1/2 tsp. dried thyme leaves
1/4 tsp. salt
1/4 tsp. pepper
1 1/2 cups shredded cheddar cheese
1 to 2 T. olive oil
 Paprika

Heat oven to 350°F. Slice tomatoes into 1/2-inch-thick slices. Combine bread crumbs, parsley, green onions, thyme, salt and pepper. In a 1 1/2-quart casserole dish, layer tomatoes, bread-crumb mixture and cheese, ending with a sprinkling of crumbs and cheese. Drizzle olive oil over top. Sprinkle with paprika. Bake covered for 30 to 35 minutes. Remove the cover during the last 10 minutes to allow browning.

Sherry Simons
Memphis, TN

Fruited Rice

Try preparing this dish with jasmine rice. This rice has a nutty flavor and complements the special almond and sesame taste.

1 cup sliced carrots
3 T. butter or margarine
2 cups diced, unpeeled apples
1 cup sliced green onions
3 cups cooked rice
½ cup raisins
1 tsp. salt
¼ tsp. pepper
¼ cup slivered almonds (optional)
1 T. sesame seeds

Sauté carrots in butter for 10 minutes or until tender-crisp. Add apples and onions. Cook 5 minutes longer. Stir in rice, raisins, salt and pepper. Cook, stirring constantly, until rice is heated through. Add almonds and sesame seeds; toss lightly.

Note Cook rice in chicken broth.

Dianne Replogle
Poland, OH

Spring Asparagus Casserole

A delightful variation to this recipe can be made by substituting brie for the Velveeta. Try preparing this dish with Black Forest or other ham for even more interest.

1 lb. fresh asparagus, cooked
2 10¾-oz. cans cream of chicken soup
½ lb. cooked ham, diced
½ lb. Velveeta cheese
6 hard-cooked eggs, sliced
½ cup milk
1 small pkg. potato chips, crushed

Heat oven to 350°F. Combine all ingredients, except potato chips, in a 2-quart casserole dish. Top with crushed potato chips. Bake uncovered for 45 minutes.

Note Thawed, frozen asparagus can be substituted for fresh.

Gordon Weichers
Steamboat Rock, IA

Marmalade Candied Carrots

Prepare these carrots with orange, lemon or ginger marmalade.

2 lbs. carrots, sliced diagonally
   (or whole, peeled baby carrots)
⅔ cup orange marmalade
3 T. spiced rum
2 T. brown sugar
2 T. butter
½ cup coarsely chopped pecans,
   toasted

Steam or simmer carrots for 10 minutes, or just until tender. Transfer to a serving dish. Stir marmalade into carrots until it is melted. Set aside and keep warm. In a saucepan, combine rum, sugar and butter. Cook over medium heat until sugar and butter are melted and smooth. Remove from heat and stir in nuts. Pour over carrots and toss to coat. Serve immediately.

David Thielbar
Grants Pass, OR

Very Special "Spuds"

Garden-fresh herbs of spring chives, sweet marjoram or sharp parsley enliven this rich and filling side dish.

5 lbs. red potatoes, peeled
8-oz. pkg. cream cheese
8-oz. pkg. sour cream
2 tsp. onion salt
2 tsp. garlic powder

3 T. butter
Salt and pepper to taste
½ cup grated sharp cheddar cheese
3 T. butter

Cook potatoes in boiling water. Drain potatoes well. Mash the potatoes until smooth. Add cream cheese, sour cream, onion salt, garlic powder, butter, salt and pepper to taste. Beat well. Place in refrigerator until ready to bake. (Recipe can be made ahead and stored in refrigerator unbaked up to 2 weeks.)

Heat oven to 350°F. Place potato mixture in a greased glass pie plate. Sprinkle with grated cheese and dot with butter. Bake for 45 minutes if baking immediately or 1 hour if taken from refrigerator.

Pat Stines
Alexander, NC

Zucchini Pie

Take this vegetable pie on picnics or pack along on outings.

2 cups chopped zucchini (1-inch
    pieces)
¼ cup chopped onion
½ cup chopped tomato
⅓ cup grated Parmesan cheese
1½ cups milk
¾ cup biscuit mix
3 eggs

Heat oven to 400°F. Layer the first four ingredients in a greased 10-inch pie plate. Beat together the milk, biscuit mix and eggs until well blended. Pour over ingredients in pie plate. Bake for 45 minutes or until browned. Serve warm or cold.

Kimberly Young
Windber, PA

Broccoli with Pasta

Try tossing with fresh quartered tomatoes, tender green beans and lots of cracked black pepper and coarse salt.

8 T. olive oil
2 T. butter
4 garlic cloves, minced
1 bunch broccoli, separated into florets
1 cup vegetable broth
1 cup fresh basil, coarsely chopped, divided
1 lb. pasta (use any shape you like: rotini, penne, etc.)
Grated cheese

In a large skillet, heat oil and butter and lightly brown the garlic. Add broccoli and stir frequently until pan gets very hot. Add vegetable broth, cover and simmer just until broccoli is tender. Add half the fresh basil and the drained hot pasta, cooked al dente, to the skillet. Mix thoroughly. Move mixture to a warm serving dish and sprinkle with grated cheese and remaining basil. Yields 4 servings.

Note Recipe may be served as a main dish accompanied by a green salad and garlic bread.

Judith Thomas
Brattleboro, VT

Oven-Roasted Rosemary Potato Wedges

There are many different varieties of potatoes available at the grocery store and more available at farmers' markets or waiting to be planted in your garden. Look for Yellow Finn, Fingerling or Red Sun to name a few varieties.

4 potatoes, unpeeled and cut into wedges
1 medium onion, finely chopped
2 cloves garlic, minced
1 T. minced fresh rosemary (or 1 tsp. crushed dried rosemary)
½ tsp. salt (optional)
¼ tsp. pepper

Heat oven to 400°F. Combine all ingredients in a large sealable plastic bag. Toss to coat potatoes, then pour into a 9 x 13-inch baking pan. Bake uncovered for 45 to 50 minutes, turning potatoes once.

JoAnn Stearns
Custer, SD

Yellow Squash Ham Bake

When served with a green salad and fresh summer fruits, this side dish can easily become the main course.

4 medium yellow squash
1 egg white
¼ cup chicken broth
1 T. fresh parsley, chopped
1 T. fresh chives, snipped
½ cup fresh lemon basil, coarsely
   chopped
1 lb. cooked ham, chopped
8-oz. pkg. grated cheddar cheese
1 cup seasoned bread crumbs, plus
   additional bread crumbs for topping
¼ to ½ cup grated Parmesan cheese

Heat oven to 325°F. Slice the squash in half and spoon out the centers; set aside. In a bowl, beat egg white with broth. Add parsley, chives and basil; mix. Add reserved squash centers; fold in ham, cheddar cheese and 1 cup bread crumbs. Fill each half of yellow squash with mixture. Place in 9 x 13-inch baking dish with just enough water to bake squash. Cover squash with Parmesan cheese and sprinkle with bread crumbs. Bake for 30 minutes until squash are tender.

Janelle McDonald
Oakdale, LA

Eggplant Parmesan

Hearty and substantial, this dish can be complemented with a curly escarole salad dressed in a light balsamic vinegar and olive oil vinaigrette.

4 eggs
4 lbs. eggplant, peeled and sliced ⅛-inch thick
4 cups bread crumbs
1½ cups olive oil
2 cups mozzarella cheese, shredded
8 oz. ricotta cheese
1 cup grated Parmesan cheese
½ cup parsley
Salt and pepper to taste
Tomato sauce

Heat oven to 375°F. Beat 2 eggs. Dredge eggplant slices in egg and then in bread crumbs. Heat olive oil and fry eggplant slices until golden brown. Drain on paper towels. Mix remaining 2 eggs in a bowl with 1 cup of the mozzarella cheese, 1 cup ricotta cheese, ½ cup of the Parmesan cheese, parsley, salt and pepper. Coat bottom of a deep lasagna pan with tomato sauce and a layer of eggplant slices, overlapping each slice by two. Continue layering eggplant slices, mozzarella cheese mixture, and the remaining ricotta. Top with tomato sauce and ½ cup Parmesan cheese. Bake for 1 hour.

Note This recipe is a great side to any meat dish or is substantial enough as a main course, too. It freezes well.

Cathy Pendergast
New Rochelle, NY

Main Dishes

Glazed Stuffed Roasting Chicken

Garnish this with colorful edible flowers, such as orange and red nasturtiums.

4- to 5-lb. roasting chicken
Cooked rice or stuffing (optional: add celery, green pepper
  and/or mushrooms to rice)
½ cup apricot jam, preserves or fresh apricot purée
¼ cup white wine, water or lemon juice
1 T. soy sauce (optional)
Flour for dusting

Heat oven to 300° to 325°F. Stuff chicken with rice or stuffing mixture. Lift the skin of the chicken breasts and legs by slicing carefully away from the meat. (Do not remove the skin.) Pierce the exposed meat with fork tines. Mix the jam, wine and soy sauce; pour this marinade over the exposed meat. Cover the marinated meat with the skin. Dust the skin lightly with flour to enhance browning. Bake in roasting pan for 30 to 35 minutes per pound. Remove skin to carve.

Mrs. Vernon Honsinger
Lexington, VA

appetizers

relishes

salads

soups

breads

side
dishes

main
dishes

desserts

Ratatouille Hash

Make this simple supper when peppers, eggplant and tomatoes are waiting to be picked in your garden.

1 lb. lean ground beef
2 cloves garlic, minced
1 T. chopped, fresh basil or 1 tsp. dried basil leaves
1 T. chopped, fresh thyme or 1 tsp. dried thyme leaves
1 large onion, sliced
1 medium green bell pepper, seeded and cut into strips
1 small eggplant, cut into 1-inch chunks
2 cups ripe tomatoes, chopped
1 tsp. salt

In a large skillet, brown beef, garlic, basil and thyme over medium heat, stirring to break up meat. Remove mixture to a dish using a slotted spoon. Set aside. Add onion, green pepper and eggplant to drippings in skillet. Sauté over medium heat for 5 minutes, or until vegetables are tender-crisp. Return beef to skillet. Add tomatoes and salt. Simmer for 10 minutes to blend flavors, stirring occasionally.

Treva Woodard
West Palm Beach, FL

Soy Sauce Chicken

This is a moist and delicious way to prepare chicken. Try boneless, skinless breasts, if you wish, and simmer for 30 minutes instead of 1 hour.

2 onions, chopped
2 slices peeled ginger root
3 T. vegetable oil
4 chicken breast halves
⅓ cup soy sauce
2 T. sugar
2 T. dry sherry
½ cup water
5 pieces star anise
Hot, cooked rice

Brown onions and gingerroot in oil in a deep skillet or Dutch oven. Add chicken and brown on both sides. Add soy sauce, sugar and sherry. Stir in water. Break up star anise and tie in cheesecloth; add to chicken. Cover and simmer for 1 hour. Serve over rice.

Betty Lou Cordi
Barton, NY

Yellow Rice and Chicken

For extra spice, add a chopped, seeded Anaheim or poblano chili pepper to this chicken recipe.

1 fryer chicken, cut up
¼ cup olive oil
1 large onion, chopped
½ green bell pepper, chopped
3 cloves garlic, minced
3½ cups water or chicken broth
4 oz. tomato sauce
1 pkg. Vigo flavoring and coloring
1 T. salt
1 tsp. dried oregano leaves
2 large bay leaves
⅛ tsp. ground cumin
2 cups uncooked long-grain
  white rice
1 cup fresh or frozen peas

In a skillet, sauté chicken pieces in olive oil until golden brown. Remove chicken from skillet. Add onion, green pepper and garlic. Sauté until onion is tender. Return chicken to skillet. Add water, tomato sauce, Vigo flavoring, salt, oregano, bay leaves and cumin. Bring to a boil. Stir in rice. Cover and reduce heat. Simmer for 25 minutes or until rice is tender. Add peas and cook until they are hot.

Dennis Lorenzo
Odessa, FL

Fusilli and Sweet Corn

Top this dish with fresh grated Parmesan cheese, or try crumbled chèvre for an interesting variation.

3 ears white or yellow corn (fresh, frozen or canned)
1 lb. fusilli
⅓ cup butter (or extra-virgin olive oil)
2 T. finely chopped, fresh chives
Salt and freshly ground pepper

In a large pot, bring 5 quarts of salted water to a boil. In the meantime, husk corn, remove silks and cut out any blemishes. Add corn to boiling water. As soon as the water starts to boil again, turn off the heat, cover the pot and let stand for 5 minutes. Remove corn with tongs and set aside until it is cool enough to handle. With a sharp knife, cut off the kernels and set aside in a warm serving dish.

Bring water back to a boil and cook fusilli until al dente. Drain pasta and transfer to bowl with corn kernels. Add butter and chives to season, salt and pepper to taste. Toss well and serve at once. Yields 6 servings.

I have also used this recipe with lemon-pepper fettuccine.

Tim Kuykendall
Springfield, IL

Venison Casserole

A moist, tender and flavorful way to prepare venison.

1 venison roast
1 onion, chopped
1 potato, peeled and chopped
1 apple, cored and chopped
1 rib celery, sliced
10¾-oz. can tomato soup
10¾-oz. can golden mushroom soup
Favorite barbecue sauce (optional)

Place roast in a slow cooker. Add onion, potato, apple and celery. Cook for 6 to 8 hours, or until venison is tender. Cut meat into small pieces or shred it. Discard vegetables and apple.

Heat oven to 325°F. Layer venison in casserole dish with undiluted soups. Top with favorite barbecue sauce, if desired. Bake for 1 hour.

Note Replace the venison roast with a beef roast if you wish.

Doris Croan
Irvington, IL

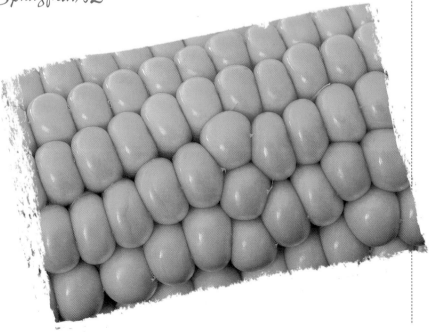

Fusilli with Sausage, Cabbage and Tomatoes

Sprinkle with freshly chopped basil to add a wonderful fragrance to this dish.

6 T. extra-virgin olive oil
1 tsp. chopped onion
1½ lbs. savory cabbage, trimmed and cut into julienne strips
6 ripe Roma tomatoes, chopped
Salt and freshly ground pepper
4 Italian sausages, cut into 1-inch chunks
1 lb. fusilli

In large frying pan, heat 3 teaspoons of olive oil over medium heat. Add onions and sauté, stirring frequently until lightly golden, about 5 minutes. Add the cabbage and continue to sauté for 2 minutes. Add the tomatoes and season to taste with salt and pepper. Stir well and cover the pan with the lid slightly ajar. Simmer over low heat, stirring occasionally, until liquid evaporates, about 40 minutes.

In a small frying pan, heat the remaining oil over medium heat. Add the sausage and cook until lightly browned. In a large pot, bring the pasta to a boil until al dente. Drain and arrange on a warm platter. Pour the cabbage sauce over the sausage and pasta; toss well. Yields 6 servings.

Tim Kuykendall
Springfield, IL

Enchiladas with Mole

Roast a variety of chili peppers and onions to serve with these enchiladas.

Mole (Mexican Gravy)

4- to 5-lb. pork loin end roast (or a cut-up chicken)
1 T. salt
½ tsp. pepper
1 3-oz. cans La Victoria Mole Poblano (dry powder mix)

Boil pork roast, salt and pepper in covered pan for several hours, or until it is tender and meat falls apart easily. Remove meat to a large bowl to cool and reserve for enchiladas. Reserve 3 cups broth for other uses. Add mole poblano to remaining broth. Mix well. Simmer, stirring occasionally, until mixture cooks down to thin gravy consistency.

Enchiladas

Vegetable oil
1 to 2 dozen corn tortillas
1 pkg. Monterey Jack or cheddar cheese, shredded
2 bunches green onions, finely chopped

Heat oven to 350°F. Shred pork meat from mole gravy. Heat 2 tablespoons oil in skillet over medium heat. With tongs, dip a tortilla into mole gravy just long enough to coat sides, then put in skillet. Heat tortilla 30 seconds per side, just long enough to soften it.

Place softened tortilla on plate and fill with a layer of meat, some cheese and a few green onions. Roll up tortilla and place seam-side-down in a 9 x 13-inch baking dish. Repeat until you have as many enchiladas as you want. Spoon mole gravy over enchiladas, then sprinkle with additional cheese and some chopped onions. Bake for 15 to 20 minutes, or until heated through and cheese is melted. Serve with Spanish rice and a salad.

Hint It is easier to make enchiladas if you have a second person to assemble them.

Mary Jane Smith
Brigham City, UT

Venison Roast à la Delores

The perfect accompaniment: topped with a spread of roasted garlic blended with herb butter.

1½- to 2-lb. venison roast
½ tsp. each: basil, garlic powder, onion powder and sage
1 bay leaf
1 onion, sliced
2 carrots, sliced
Salt and pepper to taste

Heat oven to 350°F. Mix spices together and rub over roast. Place roast in browning bag along with bay leaf, onion and carrots. Bake for 2 to 2 ½ hours until tender. Make gravy from juices in the bag. Add salt and pepper to taste.

Note Replace the venison roast with a beef roast if you wish.

Delores Meyers
Red Creek, NY

Sweet-Sour Bratwurst Skillet

A variety of roasted squash make a pretty and delicious acccompaniment.

2 T. brown sugar
2 T. vinegar
2 T. water
½ tsp. prepared mustard
¼ tsp. salt
⅛ tsp. garlic powder
Dash of pepper
8 oz. can sauerkraut, drained
Medium apple, cored and cut in wedges
½ cup sweet red or green pepper, chopped
2 T. green onion, sliced
4 fully cooked bratwurst or Polish sausage links
Snipped parsley (optional)

In skillet combine first seven ingredients. Stir in sauerkraut, apple wedges, red pepper and onion. Score brats or sausages and place atop sauerkraut mixture. Cover and simmer for 10 to 15 minutes, or until apple is tender and brats or sausages are heated through. Sprinkle with parsley, if desired. Yields 2 servings.

Tim Kuykendall
Springfield, IL

Cheese-Stuffed Chicken

A cheese and herb stuffed chicken breast is tucked inside two thin sheets of phyllo pastry.

½ cup shredded Monterey Jack cheese
½ cup shredded cheddar cheese (sharp or mild)
2 T. butter, softened
2 T. chopped, fresh parsley
2 T. chopped, fresh tarragon or 2 tsp. dried tarragon
½ tsp. black pepper
¼ tsp. salt
4 boneless, skinless chicken breast halves
8 sheets phyllo (filo) dough
¼ cup butter, melted

Heat oven to 350°F. Combine cheese, softened butter, parsley, tarragon, pepper and salt in a bowl. Beat and mash together until mixture forms a stiff paste. (Fingers work best for this.) Divide mixture into four logs about 3 inches long. Set aside.

Flatten each chicken breast by placing it between two sheets of waxed paper and pounding with a mallet. (I use a rolling pin.) Flatten to ¼ inch thick and 5 or 6 inches across. Season lightly with salt and pepper. Place a cheese log in the center of each chicken breast, then roll and fold chicken around cheese to enclose it completely.

Place a sheet of phyllo on work surface and brush lightly with melted butter. Top with a second sheet of phyllo and brush again. Place one rolled chicken breast in center of narrow edge of phyllo sheets. Roll chicken up in phyllo, tucking sides of dough in to enclose the chicken and make a neat package. Repeat with remaining phyllo and chicken rolls. Place packages, seam-side-down, in a 9 x 13-inch baking dish. Brush with any remaining butter.

Bake for 40 minutes, or until sizzling and well browned. (A meat thermometer inserted into center of chicken should read 170°F.)

Vera Arthur
Winters, CA

Stuffed Peppers

An interesting substitution for the ground pork and beef is to use fresh herb or chicken sausages.

6 green peppers
½ lb. ground beef
½ lb. ground pork
Medium onion, chopped
2 cups cooked rice
1½ tsp. salt
2 small cans tomato soup
4 cans water

Heat oven to 400°F. Cut off the tops of the peppers, remove seeds and rinse out. Mix ground beef and pork in a large bowl. Add chopped onions, rice and salt to meat and mix well. Stuff the peppers with the meat mixture, and place peppers in a large baking dish or casserole. Pour tomato soup and water over peppers. Bake for approximately 1 hour. Yields 6 servings.

Susan Meissner
Blue Ridge, GA

main dishes

107

Hot Stuffed Hungarian Peppers

Prepare this recipe with the vegetarian version of the Garden-Fresh Pasta Sauce on page 112.

12 to 18 large, hot Hungarian
    yellow peppers
1½ lbs. Italian or Polish sausage,
    removed from casings
32-oz. jar spaghetti sauce
¼ cups grated Romano or
    Parmesan cheese

Heat oven to 350°F. Cut tops off peppers and remove seeds. Stuff sausage into peppers until full. Put stuffed peppers in baking dish. Pour spaghetti sauce over peppers and sprinkle cheese over top. Cover with foil and bake for 1 hour.

Lori Capozzo
Richmond, MI

Versatile Barbecue Marinade

A barbecue marinade for Cornish game hen, chicken, lamb or beef.

2 T. butter or margarine
Water
1 small onion, coarsely chopped
½ green bell pepper, seeded and coarsely chopped
½ cup sweet-and-sour sauce
2 T. honey-mustard salad dressing
1 tsp. soy sauce
1 clove garlic, chopped or minced

In a saucepan, heat butter with a little water over medium-low heat. Add onion and pepper. Cook until the vegetables become wilted. Stir in remaining ingredients. Use marinade as follows.

1) Split Cornish hens. Add orange and/or pineapple slices to marinade. Cover hens with marinade and refrigerate for 10 hours. Remove meat from marinade and let stand at room temperature for ½ hour. Season hens with salt and pepper. Grill hens until no longer pink, basting with remaining marinade as needed.

2) Boneless, skinless chicken breasts or thighs. Cover chicken with marinade and refrigerate for 10 hours. Remove meat from marinade and let stand at room temperature for ½ hour. Season chicken with salt and pepper. Grill chicken until no longer pink, basting with remaining marinade as needed.

3) Lamb blades or chops. Cover lamb with marinade and refrigerate for 10 hours. Remove meat from marinade and let stand at room temperature for ½ hour. Season lamb with salt and pepper. Grill to desired doneness.

4) London broil. Cover meat with marinade and refrigerate for 2 hours. Remove meat from marinade and let stand at room temperature for ½ hour. Season meat with grilled steak seasoning. Grill to desired doneness.

Sandra Coykendall
Sussex, NJ

main dishes

109

Kraut Burgers

Sprinkle each kraut burger with coarse salt, pepper, sesame or herbs before baking.

2 lbs. ground beef
1 head cabbage, chopped
1 medium onion, chopped
Salt and pepper to taste
1 cup water
4 loaves frozen bread, thawed

Heat oven to 350°F. Brown beef in skillet. Add cabbage, onion, salt and pepper. Add water. Simmer for 15 minutes, or until water is nearly gone but mixture is still moist.

Divide each loaf into 3 or 4 pieces. Roll pieces into squares on floured surface. Spoon beef mixture onto squares and fold over, pinching to close. Bake for 30 minutes, or until browned.

Hint Roll out small pieces of dough to make appetizers.

Linda Lee
Pelham, AL

Appalachian Boondock Southern Fried Chicken

This country-fried chicken tastes perfect served with pickled beets and fried green tomatoes.

½ cup evaporated milk
½ cup water
3 lbs. fryer chicken, cut up
½ tsp. white lightning (optional)
1 cup all-purpose flour
2 tsp. salt
1 tsp. paprika
¼ tsp. black pepper
Vegetable oil

Combine milk and water. Dip chicken pieces in mixture. Sprinkle white lightning on dipped chicken. Combine flour, salt, paprika and pepper in paper bag. Heat ½ inch of oil in a heavy skillet until almost smoking.

Take chicken, one piece at a time, and put in paper bag. Shake to coat. Remove chicken from bag and place in skillet. Repeat with remaining chicken pieces. Brown both sides of chicken pieces. Cover tightly. Reduce heat to low and cook chicken for 40 minutes. Turn heat up to crisp chicken for 5 to 10 minutes, turning chicken pieces once. If desired, sprinkle with a little more white lightning before serving.

Delbert McCray
Roseville, OH

Southwestern Chicken Pizza

Brush each individual pizza crust with an herb or garlic olive oil to make it golden brown and crispy.

3 boneless, skinless chicken breasts
1 small onion
1 small green or red bell pepper
1½ tsp. olive oil
1 fresh sage leaf, minced
1 tsp. minced, fresh rosemary
4 individual pizza crusts
1½ cups shredded colby-jack cheese
Ranch salad dressing

Heat oven to 350°F. Cut chicken breasts into cubes. Slice onion and bell pepper into rings. Combine chicken, onion, bell pepper, oil, sage and rosemary. Sauté mixture in a skillet over medium heat until chicken is no longer pink. Arrange mixture on pizza crusts. Sprinkle shredded cheese evenly over pizzas. Bake until cheese is melted and bubbly. Slice each pizza into wedges and serve with Ranch dressing for dipping.

Diana Cei Robles
Dallas, TX

Fish Fillets in Wine Sauce

A few fresh sprigs of lemon thyme add an elegant touch.

Firm fish fillets
1 cup dry white wine
1 cup olive oil
1 medium onion
1 medium lemon
Ground nutmeg
Salt
Ground pepper

Place your favorite firm fish fillets in a casserole dish. Add dry white wine and olive oil. Finely slice the onion and lemon, and place both on the fish. Sprinkle with freshly ground nutmeg, salt and black pepper. Bake in a preheated, 350°F oven for 1 hour. Serve with parsley potatoes.

Mrs. Tillie Sanders
Grosse Pointe, MI

Garden-Fresh Pasta Sauce

Try seasoning this pasta sauce with fresh basil, thyme and oregano.

5 tomatoes, chopped
8 oz. fresh mushrooms, sliced
1 zucchini, chopped
1 onion, chopped
1/4 cup chopped, fresh parsley
1 clove garlic, minced
1 T. butter or margarine
To taste: salt, pepper, basil, thyme and oregano
6-oz. can tomato paste
Cooked, diced chicken, fish, ground beef or
    sausage (optional)

In a large pot, combine all ingredients except tomato paste and meat. Bring to a boil. Reduce heat and simmer for 30 minutes. Add tomato paste and meat. Simmer for 10 minutes longer. Serve sauce over favorite pasta.

Leslie Harder
Newcastle, WY

Great Meat Sauce

Mix this versatile sauce with rice to create a hearty filling for stuffed peppers.

1 cup olive oil
2 onions, chopped
6 cloves garlic
4 T. oregano
1 cup parsley
½ cup basil
8 cups water

10 lbs. of tomatoes, skinned
8 carrots, ground or processed
1 lb. chopped beef
1 lb. spare ribs
2 lbs. sausage (hot/sweet mixed)
4 cups red wine

Heat olive oil in a large pan. Sauté onions, garlic and herbs. Add water and tomatoes and bring to a boil. Mash tomatoes and add ground carrots. Continue cooking at a slow boil. Cover pan with fry screen to prevent splashing. Cook for approximately 1 hour when sauce begins to render down. Add chopped beef, ribs and sausage and continue to cook until desired doneness, approximately 3 to 4 hours. Add red wine in the last half hour of cooking. Yields about 4 quarts of sauce and a large bowl of meat. Recipe may be frozen for future use.

Cathy Pendergast
New Rochelle, NY

main dishes

Beef Bourguignon

**This recipe goes great over homemade mashed potatoes.
Try not peeling the potatoes before boiling and mashing.**

3 lbs. beef, cubed
1 large onion, sliced thin
½ tsp. thyme
1 bay leaf
1 T. parsley, chopped
1 clove garlic
½ tsp. salt
Freshly ground pepper
1 cup dry red wine
2 T. olive oil
¼ lb. bacon, cut in strips
18 small white onions
2 T. flour
1½ cups beef bouillon
½ lb. mushrooms
2 T. butter

Combine first ten ingredients in a large bowl and marinate for 4 hours. Fry bacon until done; add onions and sauté until tender and brown. Remove from pan. Drain and dry beef, save marinade and sauté beef in hot bacon fat, browning well. Sprinkle with flour and cook for a few minutes. Pour marinade and bouillon on beef, and bring to a simmer. Cover and cook 2 to 3 hours until beef is tender. Lightly sauté mushrooms in butter. When beef is done, add bacon, onions and mushrooms. Simmer 15 minutes. Serve over homemade mashed potatoes or egg noodles.

Brenda Simeth
Spooner, WI

Spaghetti with Shrimp Sauce

Serve this spaghetti with a sliced baguette, toasted and brushed with olive oil.

3 T. extra-virgin olive oil
1 small onion, chopped
1 lb. shrimp (prawns), peeled (may use lobster chunks or crab meat)
¾ cup dry white wine
6 ripe plum tomatoes, chopped
Salt and freshly ground pepper
1 lb. spaghetti noodles
1 T. chopped, fresh, flat-leaf parsley

In large pot, bring 5 quarts of salt water to a boil. Meanwhile, in a large frying pan, heat olive oil over low heat. Add onion and sauté until translucent. Add shrimp, raising the heat to medium, and cook for 2 minutes, stirring constantly. Add wine and continue cooking until wine evaporates, about 2 minutes. Add tomatoes and season to taste with salt and pepper. Cook for 2 more minutes.

Add spaghetti to boiling water and cook. Drain pasta and transfer to the frying pan containing the warm tomato sauce. Add parsley. Arrange on a warm platter and serve. Yields 6 servings.

Tim Knykendall
Springfield, IL

Sweet-and-Sour Baked Chicken

Tender brown rice makes a subtle, nutty accompaniment to the sweet and tangy flavors of the chicken.

¼ cup butter or margarine
½ cup chopped onion
½ cup chopped green pepper
½ cup chopped carrots
¾ cup catsup
1 cup pineapple juice
2 T. vinegar
¼ cup firm brown sugar
1 T. soy or Worcestershire sauce
½ tsp. garlic salt
½ tsp. salt
¼ tsp. black pepper
Dash of red ground pepper
Dash of ground ginger
1 cup pineapple chunks or crushed pineapple (drained)
1 to 3 lbs. cut-up chicken pieces or 8 boneless chicken breasts

Preheat oven to 400°F. In a medium skillet, heat butter until melted. Add onion, green pepper and carrots. Cook for 5 minutes, stirring. Stir in catsup, pineapple juice, vinegar, brown sugar, soy sauce, garlic salt, salt, black pepper, red pepper and ginger. Cook, stirring constantly, until mixture boils. Add pineapple chunks. Arrange chicken pieces, skin-side-up in a 9 x 13 x 2-inch baking dish. Pour the sweet-and-sour sauce over all. Bake covered for 45 minutes. Uncover and bake an additional 30 minutes.

Sandy Pocius
Sublette, IL

Broccoli Lasagna

This lasagna is great made with broccoli, but you could also try zucchini, eggplant or spinach instead.

1 large onion, diced
2 cloves garlic, minced
Olive oil
3 cups water
2 (8-oz.) cans tomato sauce
2 (6-oz.) cans tomato paste
1 cup grated Parmesan cheese,
   divided
2 T. sugar or to taste
2 tsp. dried parsley flakes, divided
1 tsp. dried oregano leaves
Salt and pepper to taste
4 cups broccoli florets and tender
   stems, cut into 1-inch pieces
1 large container cottage cheese
12 uncooked lasagna noodles
Additional grated Parmesan cheese
16 oz. mozzarella cheese, shredded

In large saucepan or skillet, sauté onion and garlic in small amount of oil (or broth or water) until tender. Add the water, tomato sauce and tomato paste; stir until smooth. Add ¼ cup Parmesan cheese, sugar, 1 teaspoon parsley, oregano, salt and pepper. Simmer for several minutes. Add broccoli and simmer until broccoli is tender, but not mushy, and sauce thickens. Set sauce aside. Combine cottage cheese, remaining ¾ cup Parmesan and 1 teaspoon parsley. Set aside.

Heat oven to 375°F. Cook noodles as directed on package. Rinse in cold water and drain. In 9 x 13-inch pan, spoon small amount of sauce into bottom of pan. Cover with 4 noodles. Spread half of cottage cheese mixture over noodles. Top with one-third of sauce. Sprinkle with light layer of Parmesan and half of mozzarella. Arrange 4 more noodles over top. Spread remaining cottage cheese mixture over noodles, then top with one-third of sauce. Arrange remaining 4 noodles over top. Top with remaining sauce, Parmesan cheese and remaining mozzarella. Bake for 30 to 45 minutes, or until bubbly and cheese is melted and golden. Let stand for 15 minutes before cutting.

L. Decker
Clymer, PA

Cheese 'n Dill Fish

This is a delicious way to prepare salmon, walleye or bass.

1 cup mayonnaise
⅓ cup grated Parmesan cheese
1 T. fresh tarragon leaves
1 T. fresh dillweed
4 fish fillets

Heat oven to 350°F. Mix together mayonnaise, Parmesan cheese, tarragon and dill weed. Spread on fish. Bake on shallow metal pan or broiler pan for 15 minutes (30 minutes for salmon steaks). Turn on broiler for a few minutes, until top is golden brown. Sprinkle with additional dillweed. Yields 4 servings.

Martha Goodfellow
Brush Prairie, WA

Desserts

Fresh Blackberry Meringue Pie

Blackberries are available from May through September depending on your region. Prepare this delicious pie when there is a bountiful harvest.

Pie
15-oz. can sweetened condensed milk
¼ cup lemon juice
2 egg yolks
3 cups blackberries, well drained
Baked pie crust, graham cracker crust
    or cookie crust

Meringue
2 egg whites
2 T. sugar
¼ tsp. salt
¼ tsp. vanilla

Heat oven to 350°F. Blend milk, lemon juice and egg yolks together. Fold in berries. Pour mixture into pie crust. For meringue, beat egg whites until stiff peaks form. Add sugar, 1 tablespoon at a time, while beating. Continue beating until shiny, moist peaks form. Beat in salt and vanilla. Spread meringue over filling, sealing to edges. Bake for 12 to 15 minutes, or until meringue is lightly browned.

Note This pie is also excellent with fresh blueberries.

Cindy Coulthurst
Minocqua, WI

appetizers

relishes

salads

soups

breads

side dishes

main dishes

desserts

Peach Cake

Refrigerate ripe peaches in a plastic bag for up to five days, bring to room temperature before using.

Cake
2 cups self-rising flour
2 cups sugar
2 eggs, slightly beaten
½ cup butter, melted
1 tsp. baking soda
1 tsp. ground cinnamon
4 ripe, fresh peaches, chopped

Sauce
½ cup evaporated milk
½ cup sugar
½ cup butter
1 tsp. vanilla

Heat oven to 350°F. Combine flour, sugar, eggs, butter, baking soda and cinnamon. Stir until smooth. Fold in peaches. Pour batter into 9 x 13-inch baking pan. Bake for 30 to 35 minutes, or until toothpick inserted in center comes out clean.

Combine all sauce ingredients. Cook for 5 minutes over medium heat, stirring often. Pour sauce over cake while hot.

Sharon Evins
Hilham, TN

Cranberry-Raspberry Pie

Prepare this pie with fresh raspberries and frozen cranberries in the summer; fresh cranberries and frozen raspberries during the cranberry season.

Pastry for a 2-crust pie
1½ cups fresh or frozen raspberries
¼ cup quick-cooking tapioca
12-oz. pkg. (3 cups) fresh or frozen cran-
* berries, coarsely chopped*
2¼ cups sugar
½ tsp. almond extract

Heat oven to 375°F. In a large bowl, combine thawed raspberries or cranberries, undrained and tapioca. Stir in fresh raspberries or cranberries, sugar and almond extract. Mix well. Let stand at room temperature for 15 minutes.

Line 9-inch pie plate with pastry crust. Pour cranberry mixture into crust. Top with remaining pastry crust and flute edges. Shield edges of pie with foil. Bake for 30 minutes. Remove foil. Bake 20 to 30 minutes longer, or until top is golden and juices and thick and clear. Serve with ice cream or whipped cream.

Mrs. John Guillou
Springfield, IL

Strawberry Pie

Prepare this pie with wild strawberries, if available, for an extra-special treat.

Crust
1½ cups all-purpose flour
½ cup vegetable oil
2 T. sugar
2 T. milk
½ tsp. salt

Filling
1 cup sugar
1 cup water
3 T. cornstarch
2 T. white corn syrup
3 T. strawberry-flavored
* gelatin mix*
Red food coloring (optional)
1 qt. fresh strawberries, hulled

Heat oven to 400°F. Mix crust ingredients well. Press dough into a 10-inch pie plate. Bake pie shell for 7 minutes, or until browned. Set aside to cool.

For filling, combine sugar, water, cornstarch and syrup in a saucepan. Bring to a boil, and cook until thick and clear, stirring constantly. Remove from heat. Stir in gelatin mix and food coloring. Add strawberries. Pour mixture into cooled pie shell. Chill until set.

Hint Recipe can be multiplied 1½ times and made in a 9 x 13-inch pan.

Kathy Vandenberg
Green Bay, WI

Heirloom Red Currant Pie

Fresh currants are in season June through August. Pick or select the brilliant red currants while they are plump and without hulls. Currants can be refrigerated for four days, or frozen and used throughout the year.

1 cup mashed currants
1 cup sugar
1 cup water
2 T. cornstarch
2 egg yolks
1 T. butter
1 tsp. vanilla
Baked pie shell
Meringue

Heat oven to 325°F. In a saucepan, mix currants, sugar, water and cornstarch together. Stir in egg yolks. Cook mixture over medium heat until thickened, stirring constantly. Add butter and vanilla, stirring until butter is melted. Pour mixture into pie shell. Top with meringue. Bake for 15 minutes, or until meringue is lightly browned.

Barbara Cogburn
Clyde, NC

Rhubarb Crisp

Serve with whipped cream flavored with the zest of orange peel.

Rhubarb Mixture
1 cup sugar
3 T. uncooked tapioca
3 cups chopped rhubarb

Topping
1 cup sugar
1 cup all-purpose flour
1 egg, beaten
1 tsp. baking powder
½ tsp. salt

Heat oven to 350°F. Combine sugar and tapioca. Spread rhubarb in pan. Sprinkle sugar mixture over top. Put pan in oven while preparing topping.

Combine all topping ingredients. Spoon mixture over rhubarb. Bake for 30 minutes, or until browned.

Elizabeth Everitt
Lake Elmo, MN

Carameled Dumplings

Serve these dumplings with slices of crisp apple, juicy pear or tart berries.

Caramel
1 cup sugar, divided
2 cups hot water
2 T. butter
1/4 tsp. salt

Dumplings
1 1/2 cups all-purpose flour
1/2 cup sugar
1/2 cup milk
2 T. butter
2 tsp. baking powder
1/2 tsp. vanilla

In a heavy saucepan, cook 1/2 cup sugar until it begins to caramelize. Add remaining 1/2 cup sugar and the remaining caramel ingredients. Cook and stir until sugar is dissolved and mixture is smooth. Keep warm.

Combine all dumpling ingredients. Mix lightly. Drop mixture by spoonfuls into hot caramel sauce to make 10 dumplings. Cook over low heat, covered, for 20 minutes. Serve hot or warm, either plain or with cream.

Darlene Frick
International Falls, MN

Easy Peanut Butter Cookies

Simple to make and delicious to eat, these cookies taste especially good eaten with a wedge of juicy fruit.

1 cup peanut butter (chunky or smooth)
1 cup sugar
2 cups flour
1 egg
1 tsp. vanilla

Heat oven to 350°F. Mix all ingredients well. Form into balls. Place balls 2 inches apart on ungreased baking sheet. Mash each ball in a criss-cross pattern with a fork. Bake for 8 to 10 minutes, or until edges start to brown.

Penny Clyburn
Vinton, VA

Dutch Oatmeal Bars

Apples, plums, peaches or nectarines make perfect complements to these bars.

Bars

1½ cups boiling water
1 cup quick-cooking oatmeal
1 cup brown sugar
1 cup granulated sugar
½ cup vegetable shortening
2 eggs, beaten
1½ cups all-purpose flour
1 tsp. baking soda
½ tsp. ground cinnamon
½ tsp. salt
½ tsp. vanilla

Frosting

1 cup shredded coconut
½ cup brown sugar
½ cup chopped nuts
6 T. margarine, melted
½ tsp. vanilla

Heat oven to 350°F. Pour boiling water over oatmeal. Stir to combine, then set aside to cool. In a mixing bowl, cream sugars, shortening and eggs together. In a separate bowl, combine flour, baking soda, cinnamon and salt. Stir flour mixture and vanilla into sugar mixture. Add oatmeal and mix well.

Pour batter into a greased 9 x 13-inch baking pan. Set aside. Combine all frosting ingredients. Spoon frosting over batter in pan. Bake for 45 to 50 minutes.

Bonnie Schuh
Williams, MN

Fresh Coconut Cake

Choose a coconut that is heavy for its size and sounds full of liquid when shaken.

1 coconut

Cake
1½ cups sugar
¾ cup margarine, softened
4 eggs, separated
2¼ cups all-purpose flour
½ cup water
¼ cup coconut milk
2¼ tsp. baking powder
1½ tsp. coconut extract

Frosting
1½ cups sugar
½ cup water or coconut milk
4 egg whites
½ tsp. cream of tartar

Heat oven to 350°F. Bake coconut for 20 to 25 minutes, or until shell cracks. Remove outer shell—it comes off easier when coconut is still warm. Pierce coconut twice and drain milk. Peel off inner "shell," then shred coconut. Set aside.

Heat oven to 350°F. Cream together sugar, margarine and egg yolks. Mix in remaining cake ingredients, except egg whites. Beat egg whites to stiff peaks, then fold into batter. Pour batter into one 9 x 13-inch pan or two 8-inch round pans that have been sprayed with nonstick cooking spray. Bake for 35 to 40 minutes, or until a toothpick inserted in center of cake comes out clean. (Optional: If your coconut has plenty of milk, spoon some over the baked cake.)

For frosting, combine sugar and water in a saucepan. Boil until temperature is between hard and soft ball stage on a candy thermometer. Beat egg whites with cream of tartar to stiff peaks. Add hot sugar water to egg whites. Beat for 1 minute. (Do not overbeat!) Frost cake and cover with shredded coconut (If making a layer cake, sprinkle coconut between layers.)

Mrs. William Schrock
Stuarts Draft, VA

Easy Peach Custard Pie

Freeze fresh peaches in season to use when preparing this recipe at other times of the year.

6 ripe, fresh peaches, peeled and
*   sliced*
1 unbaked 9-inch pie shell
2 eggs
1 cup sugar
¼ cup all-purpose flour
1 cup heavy cream
1 tsp. vanilla

Heat oven to 375°F. Place peaches in pie shell. Beat eggs lightly in a bowl, then blend in sugar and flour. Stir in cream and vanilla. Pour mixture over peaches. Bake pie for 40 to 50 minutes, or until set. Serve warm or chilled. Refrigerate any leftovers.

JoAnn Stearns
Custer, SD

Sunflower Seed Cookies

Pack these cookies along for a walk, a bike ride or a drive through the country.

1 cup vegetable shortening
1 cup light brown sugar
1 cup granulated sugar
2 large eggs
3 cups uncooked rolled oats
1½ cups all-purpose flour
1½ cups salted sunflower seeds
½ cup chopped, unsalted peanuts
  or raisins
1 tsp. baking soda

Heat oven to 350°F. Cream shortening and sugars together until smooth. Beat in eggs. Stir in remaining ingredients. Drop cookie dough by teaspoons on ungreased cookie sheets. Bake for 10 to 12 minutes, or until cookies are light golden brown.

*Regina Gambino
Hamburg, NY*

Persimmon Pudding

Persimmons can be used in baked goods, puddings and other desserts, as well as eaten out of hand. They contain a good amount of Vitamin A and some Vitamin C.

2 cups persimmon pulp
2 cups sugar
2 eggs
1 cup buttermilk
1 tsp. baking soda
¼ cup margarine, melted
1¾ cups all-purpose flour
1 tsp. baking powder
½ tsp. salt
1 cup milk

Heat oven to 350°F. In large bowl, combine persimmon pulp, sugar and eggs. In separate bowl, combine buttermilk and baking soda, then add to pulp mixture. Stir in melted margarine.

In third bowl, combine flour, baking powder and salt. Add flour mixture to the pulp mixture alternately with milk. Pour batter into 9 x 13-inch baking pan. Bake for 55 to 60 minutes. Serve plain or with whipped cream.

Note Use the American Wild Persimmon, not the Oriental, for this recipe.

Nadine McCracken
Brownsburg, IN

Zucchini Cake

Create flower and garden stencils draw the design on paper, cut it out and use it as a pattern. Sift powdered sugar through the stencil to decorate the cake.

2 cups sugar
1 cup margarine or shortening
1 tsp. grated orange peel (optional)
1 tsp. ground cinnamon
½ tsp. ground allspice
½ tsp. ground nutmeg
3 eggs
2 cups finely shredded zucchini
⅔ cup chopped nuts
3 cups all-purpose flour
2 tsp. baking powder
1 tsp. baking soda
½ tsp. salt

Heat oven to 350°F. Cream sugar and margarine together until light and fluffy. Beat in orange peel and spices. Beat in eggs. Stir in zucchini and nuts. Combine remaining ingredients and stir into sugar mixture.

Grease and flour two 9-inch round cake pans or one 9 x 13-inch pan. Pour batter into pans (or pan). Bake for 35 to 40 minutes, or until cake pulls from the sides of pan.

Note To make muffins instead of cake, cut the baking time to 10 to 15 minutes.

Diana Ranslam
Independence, OR

Five Freeze

Pour this mixture in a pan to freeze, or spoon mixture into lemon, orange and lime halves before freezing. Another idea is to spoon mixture into popsicle molds. Use licorice root for natural sticks.

3 bananas, peeled and sliced
1 small can crushed pineapple, undrained
1 cup orange juice
½ cup sugar
Juice of 3 lemons

Combine all ingredients in a blender. Process until smooth. Pour mixture into a pan and freeze. When ready to serve, cut into small squares.

Peggy Lee Payne
Lexington, VA

Chocolate Zucchini Tube Cake

Serve this cake with a whipped cream topping. For a double chocolate cake, fold ½ cup melted chocolate chips into 1 cup whipped cream, then top the cake.

2½ cups all-purpose flour
½ cup unsweetened cocoa
2½ tsp. baking powder
1½ tsp. baking soda
1 tsp. ground cinnamon
1 tsp. salt
2 cups sugar
¾ cup butter or margarine
2 eggs
2 tsp. orange juice
2 tsp. vanilla
½ cup milk
2 cups shredded zucchini

Heat oven to 350°F. In a bowl, combine flour, cocoa, baking powder, baking soda, cinnamon and salt. In a separate bowl, cream sugar and butter together until light and fluffy. Beat in eggs, orange juice and vanilla. Beat in flour mixture alternately with milk. Stir in zucchini. Pour into greased tube pan. Bake for 1 hour, or until browned and a toothpick inserted in center comes out clean. Serve cake with whipped cream or ice cream.

Karen Grimm
Cologne, MN

Rhubarb Crumb Cake

A rhubarb spice cake with a sweet coconut topping.

Cake
2 eggs
½ cup vegetable oil
⅓ cup milk
2 cups sifted all-purpose flour
1½ cups sugar
1 tsp. baking soda
1 tsp. ground cinnamon
1 tsp. salt
¼ tsp. ground allspice
2 cups fresh or frozen rhubarb pieces (½-inch pieces)

Topping
⅔ cup all-purpose flour
½ cup brown sugar
¼ cup margarine
¾ cup flaked coconut
¼ cup chopped nuts

Heat oven to 350°F. Beat together eggs, oil and milk. Add flour, sugar, baking soda, cinnamon, salt and allspice. Stir in rhubarb. Pour into a greased and floured 9 x 13-inch pan.

For topping, blend flour, sugar and margarine together until mixture is crumbly. Stir in coconut and chopped nuts. Sprinkle topping over cake batter. Bake for 40 minutes, or until toothpick inserted in center comes out clean.

Jean Hitchcock
Dover Foxcroft, ME

Blueberry Cobbler

Make this cobbler with blueberries, peaches or nectarines.

2 cups sugar, divided
¾ cup all-purpose flour
¾ cup milk
2 tsp. baking powder
⅛ tsp. salt
½ cup butter
2 cups fresh blueberries

Heat oven to 350°F. Combine 1 cup sugar, the flour, milk, baking powder and salt. Melt butter in an 8-inch square baking pan. Pour batter over melted butter. Do not stir. Mix blueberries with remaining 1 cup sugar. Spoon berries over batter. Bake for 1 hour, or until browned. Serve warm with whipped cream or ice cream.

Edward Hankinson
Aiken, SC

desserts

129

Pumpkin Roll

Sprinkle this cream cheese pumpkin roll with powdered sugar and nutmeg.

3 eggs
1 cup granulated sugar
⅔ cup cooked mashed pumpkin
1 tsp. lemon juice
¾ cup all-purpose flour

2 tsp. ground cinnamon
1¼ tsp. ground ginger
1¼ tsp. ground nutmeg
1 tsp. baking powder
½ tsp. salt

1¼ cups powdered sugar, divided
8-oz. pkg. cream cheese, softened
¼ cup butter, softened
½ tsp. vanilla

Heat oven to 375°F. Beat eggs at high speed with electric mixer for 5 minutes. Gradually add granulated sugar, beating well. Stir in pumpkin and lemon juice. Combine flour, cinnamon, ginger, nutmeg, baking powder and salt. Add to pumpkin mixture and blend well.

Spoon batter into a greased and floured 15 x 10 x 1-inch jelly roll pan, spreading evenly to corners of pan. Bake for 15 minutes, or until toothpick inserted in center comes out clean. Turn cake onto a lint-free towel sprinkled with

¼ cup powdered sugar. Beginning at short end, roll up cake and towel together, jelly-roll fashion. Let cool.

Combine remaining 1 cup powdered sugar, cream cheese, butter and vanilla. Beat until smooth and creamy. Unroll cake and spread with filling. Roll cake up again, without the towel. Chill seam-side-down.

Crystal Bowden
Colonial Heights, VA

Come-Back Cake

A beautiful torte layered with spiced apples and apple butter.

1 lb. dried, tart apples
2 cups sugar, divided
2 tsp. ground cinnamon
½ tsp. ground cloves
½ tsp. ground allspice
4 cups all-purpose flour
4 tsp. baking powder
1 tsp. salt
½ tsp. baking soda
1 cup buttermilk
½ cup butter, melted
2 eggs
2 tsp. vanilla
1 cup apple butter

Cook apples until tender. Mash thoroughly. Add 1 cup sugar, cinnamon, cloves and allspice. Set apple mixture aside and cool.

Heat oven to 450°F. In a bowl, combine remaining 1 cup sugar, flour, baking powder, salt and baking soda. Add remaining ingredients, mixing to form a soft dough. Divide dough into 6 portions. Dough will be wet. Roll out each portion, using enough flour to prevent sticking. (Portions will resemble big pancakes.)

Bake dough in 9-inch round cake pans until slightly brown. Cool. Spread each layer with apple mixture, then a thin layer of apple butter, stacking layers as you go. (Do not put apples on top layer.) Place cake in covered container for 12 hours before cutting.

Betty Potter
Mt. Carmel, IL

Irish Apple Cake

Wrap this cake in cheesecloth to give as a gift. As a part of the gift, give pint size baskets of blackberries.

3 cups all-purpose flour
1 cup sugar
1 cup packed brown sugar
2 tsp. baking soda
1 tsp. ground cinnamon
1 tsp. salt
3 cups diced apples
1¼ cups vegetable oil
2 eggs
1 cup chopped walnuts (optional)
Shredded coconut (optional)

Heat oven to 350°F. Combine all dry ingredients. Add apples, oil, eggs, walnuts and coconut. Mix well. (Mixture will be crumbly.) Press mixture into tube pan. Bake for 1 to 1½ hours, or until browned and toothpick inserted in center comes out clean.

Kimberly Hartshorn
Cincinnati, OH

Fresh Rhubarb Pie

Bake a ginger rhubarb pie for am interesting variation; simply add 1 tablespoon of grated fresh gingerroot.

Pastry for a 2-crust pie
1½ to 1⅔ cups sugar
⅓ cup all-purpose flour
½ tsp. grated orange peel (optional)
4 cups cut-up rhubarb (½-inch pieces)
2 T. margarine or butter

Heat oven to 425°F. Line 9-inch pie plate with pastry crust. Combine sugar, flour and orange peel. Spoon half of the rhubarb into pie crust. Sprinkle with half of sugar mixture. Repeat with remaining rhubarb and sugar mixture. Dot with margarine. Top with remaining pastry crust. Flute edges and cut slits in top. Sprinkle sugar on top, if desired.

Cover edge of crust with foil to prevent excessive browning. Bake for 40 to 50 minutes, or until pie is browned and juice begins to bubble through slits in crust. (Remove foil during last 10 minutes of baking.)

Tami Juchemich
Negaunee, MI

Rhubarb Pudding

A scoop of homemade ice cream spiced with nutmeg is a delicious addition to this dessert.

Pudding

2 cups fresh or frozen rhubarb, cut into pieces
1 cup sugar
1 cup crushed pineapple, drained
1 egg, beaten
2 T. self-rising flour
2 T. lemon juice (optional)

Topping

1 cup self-rising flour
½ cup margarine
½ cup sugar

Heat oven to 350°F. Combine rhubarb, sugar, pineapple, egg, flour and lemon juice in mixing bowl. Mix well. Pour into 9 or 10-inch square baking dish. Combine topping ingredients, mixing until small grains are formed. Spread topping over rhubarb mixture. Bake for 55 minutes.

David Hutchison
Monticello, KY

Hot Water Gingerbread

Add 1 tablespoon of grated fresh ginger and 1 teaspoon black pepper to this recipe for a spiced gingerbread treat.

Bread
1 cup all-purpose flour
½ cup sugar
1 tsp. salt
1 tsp. ground ginger
½ tsp. baking soda
½ cup molasses
½ cup hot water
1 egg
1 T. margarine

Topping
2 T. sugar
2 tsp. ground cinnamon

Whipped cream

Heat oven to 350°F. Combine dry ingredients. Set aside. In bowl, beat molasses, hot water, egg and margarine together. Gradually stir hot water mixture into flour mixture. Beat for 1 minute. Pour batter into greased 8-inch square pan. Combine topping ingredients and sprinkle over top. Bake for 25 minutes, or until toothpick inserted in center comes out clean. Cool before cutting. Top with whipped cream.

Marcella West (Moore)
Washington, IL

Best Apple Crisp

Take a day trip to an apple orchard and pick a variety of apples. Treat yourself to homebaked apple crisp when you arrive home.

6 to 7 cups sliced, peeled apples
1 cup sugar
1 tsp. baking powder
¾ tsp. salt
1 egg
¼ cup butter, melted
Ground cinnamon

Heat oven to 350°F. Spread apples in an oblong glass baking dish that has been sprayed with nonstick cooking spray. Combine sugar, baking powder and salt. Mix in egg until crumbly and sprinkle over apples. Drizzle melted butter over all. Sprinkle cinnamon over top. Bake for 30 to 40 minutes, or until browned and apples are tender. Serve with whipped topping or ice cream.

Nettie Eytzen
Delft, MN

Pumpkin Spice Cake

Grow pie pumpkins in the pumpkin patch. Bake a pumpkin and scoop out the pulp to make this cake.

Cake

2 cups all-purpose flour
2 cups cooked or canned pumpkin
1¼ cups sugar
1 cup chopped nuts
½ cup vegetable oil
⅓ cup water
1¼ tsp. baking soda
1 tsp. salt
1 tsp. ground cinnamon
1 tsp. ground cloves
1 tsp. ground nutmeg
1 tsp. vanilla
3 eggs

Frosting

8-oz. pkg. cream cheese, softened
1 T. milk
1 tsp. vanilla
4 cups powdered sugar

Heat oven to 350°F. Grease and flour 9 x 13-inch baking pan. Combine all cake ingredients and beat at low speed with electric mixer for 1 minute, scraping bowl frequently. Beat at medium speed for 2 minutes. Pour batter into prepared pan.

Bake cake for 45 to 50 minutes, or until toothpick inserted in center comes out clean. Cool on wire rack. For frosting, beat cream cheese, milk and vanilla in medium bowl at low speed with electric mixer until smooth. Beat in powdered sugar, 1 cup at a time, until smooth and spreadable. Spread frosting on cooled cake.

Sandra Washa
Brule, NE

Mother Monsen's Tea Cakes

Sprinkle these tea cake triangles with powdered sugar. Try covering half the tea cake with paper so that only half the triangle gets the sprinkling of sugar.

1 lb. unsalted butter, softened
2 cups sugar
4 eggs
2 cups all-purpose flour
1 tsp. vanilla
½ cup chopped, blanched almonds
¼ cup dried currants

Heat oven to 375°F. Lightly grease a 12 x 18-inch jelly-roll pan with 1 teaspoon of the butter. Set aside. Cream remaining butter and sugar together. Beat in eggs, one at a time. Add flour and vanilla. Mix well. Spread mixture in the prepared pan. Sprinkle with almonds and currants; press lightly.

Bake for 20 to 25 minutes, or just until edges are golden brown. Cool cake in pan. Cut cake into 3-inch squares, then cut each square into 2 triangles. Store in airtight container. (These also freeze well.)

Note Do *not* substitute margarine for butter in this recipe!

Susan Stitch
Florissant, MO

Green Tomato Pie

A great way to use up all those green tomatoes!

Pastry for a 2-crust pie
1 cup sugar
½ cup all-purpose flour
Green tomatoes
Butter
1 T. white vinegar
Ground cinnamon

Heat oven to 400°F. Line 9-inch pie plate with pastry crust. Combine sugar and flour. Sprinkle mixture over bottom of crust. Peel and thinly slice enough green tomatoes to fill pie plate. Dot tomatoes with butter. Sprinkle vinegar and cinnamon over tomatoes.

Top pie with second crust and seal edges. Sprinkle a little sugar over top crust. Bake for 15 minutes at 400°F. Reduce heat to 350°F. Bake 35 minutes longer, or until golden brown. Serve warm.

Charlotte Downey
Shoshoni, WY

Moonpies

For variety, prepare these moonpies with any dried fruit. Figs, apricots, mango and dates are delicious to combine with the apples.

4 cups dried apples
Water
Sugar to taste
Ground cinnamon to taste
Pie crust dough
Milk

In a saucepan, combine apples with just enough water to prevent scorching. Cook over medium heat until apples are soft. Run apples through a food mill. Stir in sugar and cinnamon to your taste. Let filling cool. (I make mine a day ahead.)

Heat oven to 400°F. Roll a small piece of pie crust dough into a 4-inch circle. Fold back a third of the circle and mark with a pastry cutter, then open again. Add some filling. Fold dough circle double, then trim around. Prick moonpie with a fork. Repeat with remaining dough and filling. Brush moonpies lightly with milk. Bake until golden brown.

Cindy Cox
Hustontown, PA

Sally Lunn Cookies

These cookies can be sandwiched together with frosting, leaving the top unfrosted.

Cookies
1 cup margarine
1½ cup sugar
1 cup molasses
½ cup black coffee
½ tsp. ginger
½ tsp. nutmeg
¼ tsp. cloves
2 tsp. baking soda
5½ to 6 cups flour

Frosting
1 cup sugar
1 cup water
1 package unflavored gelatin
Dash of salt
2 cups powdered sugar

Heat oven to 350°F. Blend together margarine and sugar. Add molasses and coffee; stir well. Blend in ginger, nutmeg, cloves, soda and flour. Chill dough. Roll ¼-inch thick. Cut into rectangles. (I use a Spam can.) Place on cookie sheet and bake 6 to 8 minutes.

Make frosting by mixing sugar, water, gelatin and salt in a saucepan. Bring to a boil and simmer for 10 minutes. Pour this syrup over 2 cups of powdered sugar. Beat at high speed for 10 minutes, or until frosting is spreading consistency. Spread generous amount on each cookie. Dry 5 to 6 hours before placing in airtight container.

Sharon Walker
Medford, MN

Cherry Custard Pie

Make this pie with a pudding mix, or prepare a homemade pudding to add to the special treat of a homebaked cherry pie.

1 pkg. vanilla pudding mix
1 1/2 cups milk
Baked 9-inch pie shell
1 lb. fresh or frozen pitted sour cherries
1/2 cup cherry juice
1/2 cup sugar
3 T. cornstarch
1 T. vegetable shortening
Red food coloring

In a saucepan, add milk slowly to pudding mix and blend well. Cook until mixture is thick. Pour into baked pie shell. Cover with cherries. In a saucepan, combine cherry juice, sugar and cornstarch. Boil for 2 minutes, or until thick, stirring constantly. Stir in shortening until melted. Brighten color with a few drops food coloring. Pour over cherries. Chill until set. Garnish with baked pastry cherries, if desired.

Anna Clark
Painted Post, NY

Holiday Fruit Pie

Adorn this pie for the holidays with an herb wreath made with rosemary and thyme. Sugared cranberries accent the wreath.

Crust
1 cup all-purpose flour
1/2 cup cold unsalted butter,
    cut into small pieces
1/4 tsp. salt
3 to 4 T. ice water

Filling
1 cup raisins
1 cup golden raisins
1 cup dried cranberries
1 cup finely diced apple
1/2 cup sugar
1/2 cup each: dried peaches, apricots and pineapple
1/2 cup chopped walnuts
1 medium seedless orange, unpeeled, finely chopped
1/2 cup brandy or rum
2 T. tapioca
2 T. lemon juice
1/2 tsp. each: ground cinnamon, cloves, cardamom and
    nutmeg

Heat oven to 400°F. For crust, combine flour, butter and salt. Place in food processor fitted with a steel blade. Pulse until mixture resembles coarse crumbs. Add ice water, one tablespoon at a time, pulsing as you add, until the dough is well mixed and clings together in a ball. Divide dough in half and roll out one ball on floured surface. Fit crust into pie plate. Set aside.

Combine all filling ingredients and mix well. Spoon into pie crust. Roll out second piece of dough for top crust. Top pie with second crust, flute edges and cut slits in top. Bake for 35 to 45 minutes. (Cover edges of crust with foil if they begin to get too brown.)

Cris Liotta
Imperial Beach, CA

Rhubarb Crunch

Fold ¼ cup chopped crystalline ginger into whipping cream or softened ice cream to accompany this dessert.

Topping

1 cup sifted all-purpose flour
1 cup packed brown sugar
¾ cup uncooked rolled oats
½ cup butter or margarine, melted
1 tsp. ground cinnamon

Rhubarb Mixture

4 cups diced rhubarb
1 cup sugar
1 cup water
2 T. cornstarch
1 tsp. vanilla

Heat oven to 350°F. Combine all topping ingredients until crumbly. Press half mixture in bottom of 9-inch pie pan. Spread rhubarb over top. In small saucepan, combine sugar, water, cornstarch and vanilla. Cook over medium heat, stirring until thick and clear. Pour mixture over rhubarb. Sprinkle remaining topping mixture over top. Bake for 1 hour. Serve warm with whipped topping, ice cream or just plain.

Jo Ann Daeda
Hermantown, MN

Banapple Pie

The best pies are made with a variety of apples. Haralson and Cortland apples are a perfect combination. Take a trip to a local farmers' market to find heirloom varieties.

Pastry for a 2-crust pie
3 T. all-purpose flour
2 to 4 T. sugar
3/8 tsp. ground cinnamon
1/4 tsp. vanilla
Dash of salt
3 to 4 medium apples of your choice, thinly sliced
3 to 4 very ripe bananas, thinly sliced
3 T. margarine
1/8 tsp. lemon juice

Heat oven to 425°F. Line 9-inch pie plate with pastry crust. Combine flour, sugar, cinnamon, vanilla and salt. Stir in apples and bananas until well mixed. Spoon mixture into prepared pastry shell. Dot with margarine and sprinkle with lemon juice. Top with remaining pastry crust and seal edges. Cut slits in top. Cover edges with foil.

Place pie on baking sheet to catch any overspill. Bake for 40 to 50 minutes, or until mixture bubbles through slits in crust. Remove foil during last 15 minutes of baking time. Cool pie on cooling rack.

Note This recipe uses very little sugar. My husband is a diabetic and came up with this twist on apple pie out of desperation.

*Susan Novello
Leland, NC*

Banana Cake

This cake can be baked in two 8-inch cake pans. Slice an extra banana and place between the layers on top of the frosting. Sprinkle with zest of lemon.

Cake
2 1/4 cups all-purpose flour
1 1/4 cups sugar
1 1/2 tsp. baking soda
1 tsp. salt
1/2 cup vegetable shortening
1/2 cup sour milk or buttermilk
2 eggs
2 ripe bananas
1 tsp. vanilla

Frosting
1/4 cup butter, softened
1 small ripe banana
1 tsp. lemon juice
3 cups powdered sugar
Milk, if necessary

Heat oven to 350°F. Combine flour, sugar, baking soda and salt. Add shortening, milk, eggs, bananas and vanilla. Beat at medium speed with electric mixer for 2 minutes. Pour batter into greased 9 x 13-inch baking pan. Bake for 30 to 35 minutes, or until toothpick inserted in center comes out clean. Cool.

For frosting, combine butter, banana and lemon juice. Beat in powdered sugar until smooth, adding a little milk if necessary for a smooth frosting. Frost cooled cake.

*Jean Soebbing
Forest Lake, MN*

desserts

Grandma's Stuff

You can make this cake with most any fruit; just make sure it's fresh, ripe and juicy.

1 cup all-purpose flour
1 cup sugar
1 cup milk
1 T. baking powder
Pinch of salt
3 cups fruit of choice with juice

Heat oven to 350°F. Combine all ingredients, except fruit. Pour batter into greased 8-inch square pan. Pour fruit and juice over batter. Bake for 1¼ hours, or until batter comes to the top and browns.

Note Recipe can be doubled and baked in a 9 x 13-inch baking pan.

Shirley Pennington
Ironton, MO

Rhubarb Coffee Cake

For special occasions, serve this cake with fresh strawberries as a topping.

Cake
1½ cups packed brown sugar
½ cup margarine
1 egg
1 tsp. vanilla
2 cups all-purpose flour
1 cup buttermilk
1 tsp. baking soda
Dash of salt
2 cups diced fresh rhubarb

Topping
½ cup sugar
½ cup chopped pecans
1½ tsp. margarine
1 tsp. ground cinnamon

Heat oven to 350°F. Cream sugar, margarine, egg and vanilla together. Add flour, buttermilk, baking soda and salt. Mix well. Fold in rhubarb. Pour into greased 9 x 13-inch baking pan. Combine all topping ingredients and sprinkle over batter. Bake for 40 to 45 minutes, or until toothpick inserted in center comes out clean.

Note Do not use frozen rhubarb for this recipe.

Marcella West (Moore)
Washington, IL

Strawberry Upside-Down Cake

Try serving this cake with a fresh strawberry purée. Blend 1 pint strawberries with 2 T. grated orange peel and ¼ cup sugar, and drizzle over the top.

1 cup sugar
3 T. butter, softened
2 large eggs
1 tsp. vanilla
2 cups flour
½ tsp. salt
2 tsp. baking powder
1 cup milk
1 pint strawberries, stemmed and
    halved
1 T. butter, softened
¼ cup sugar

Heat oven to 350°F. Mix sugar and butter; add eggs and vanilla and mix well. Sift together flour, salt and baking powder. Alternating with milk, add flour mixture to sugar mixture. Pour into greased 1½-quart baking mold or 8-inch baking pan. Place strawberries on top of the batter until entire cake is covered.

Make topping by mixing butter and sugar together. Mix with your fingers and sprinkle on top of strawberries. Bake for 1 hour or until toothpick inserted in center comes out clean.

Note Other fruits may be used in place of the strawberries or the batter alone can be used for cupcakes.

Bette Carmer
Squaw Valley, CA

Mile High Frozen Pie

This is a fun dessert to make with the strawberries that were picked during the season and frozen for a sampling of summer throughout the year.

2 egg whites
10-oz. pkg. frozen strawberries,
   partially thawed
1 cup sugar
1½ tsp. lemon juice
½ tsp. salt
1 cup heavy
   whipping cream
1 tsp. vanilla
Prepared pie shell

Beat egg whites until stiff peaks form. Add strawberries, sugar, lemon juice and salt. Beat mixture for 20 minutes at high speed with electric mixer. Whip cream and vanilla in separate bowl. Fold whipped cream into strawberry mixture. Mound mixture into pie shell and freeze.

Alice Gifford
Lafayette, IN

Raisin Pfeffernüesse

Try making these cookies with dried cranberries, cherries or apricots in place of the raisins.

15-oz. box raisins
1 cup blanched almonds
½ cup cut-up candied fruit
2 cups all-purpose flour
2 tsp. ground cinnamon
1 tsp. ground cloves
½ tsp. baking powder
½ tsp. baking soda
½ tsp. salt
½ tsp. freshly ground pepper
2 cups packed light brown sugar
3 eggs
Powdered sugar

With fine blade of food grinder or in a food processor, grind raisins, almonds and fruit together. Set aside. Combine flour, cinnamon, cloves, baking powder, baking soda, salt and pepper. Stir into raisin mixture. In large bowl of electric mixer, beat brown sugar and eggs until fluffy. Stir into raisin mixture and mix well. (Dough will be stiff.) Chill at least 1 hour.

Heat oven to 350°F. With floured hands, form dough into 1-inch balls and place 2 inches apart on well-greased baking sheet. Bake for 10 minutes, or until cookies are brown on bottom but still soft on top. Remove cookies to cooling rack. While still warm, shake cookies in bag with powdered sugar to coat them. Cool completely and store in airtight container at least 1 week before eating.

Katie Ruimerman
Middletown, CT

Never-Fail Carrot Cake

To serve a wedge of this cake without frosting, sprinkle it with powdered sugar and a dash of cardamom.

2 cups all-purpose flour
2 tsp. baking soda
1½ tsp. baking powder
1 tsp. salt
2 tsp. ground allspice
1½ tsp. ground cardamom (optional)
1 cup packed light brown sugar
1 cup granulated sugar
1 cup vegetable oil
4 large eggs
2 cups carrots, shredded (about 4 medium-size)
8-oz. can crushed pineapple, drained
1 cup walnut pieces, chopped
Cream cheese frosting

Heat oven to 350°F. Grease a 9 x 13-inch baking pan. Mix flour, baking soda, baking powder, salt, allspice and cardamom in a large bowl and set aside. In a medium-size bowl beat sugars, oil and eggs with a wooden spoon until blended. Stir sugar mixture into flour mixture, and beat with wooden spoon for 1 minute. Stir in carrots, pineapple and nuts until blended. Pour into prepared pan. Bake for 30 to 35 minutes or until toothpick inserted in center comes out clean. Cool completely in pan on rack. Spread frosting on top.

June F. Blue
Wadena, IA

Sour Cream Apple Pie

To turn this pie into a tart simply place pastry in a 9-inch tart pan. During blackberry season, mix 1 pint hand-picked blackberries with the apples.

Pastry for single-crust pie
5 large tart apples
1 T. lemon juice
¾ cup sugar
⅓ cup all-purpose flour
1 tsp. ground cinnamon
¼ tsp. salt
¼ tsp. ground nutmeg
¼ cup butter
½ cup sour cream

Heat oven to 400°F. Line 9-inch pie pan with pastry crust. Peel apples and cut into thick slices. Arrange slices in overlapping rows in pie pan. Sprinkle with lemon juice. Mix sugar, flour, cinnamon, salt and nutmeg in a bowl. Cut in butter until crumbly. Spoon mixture over apples. Spread sour cream over top. Bake for 25 minutes. Reduce oven temperature to 350°F. Bake for 20 to 25 minutes longer, or until apples are tender.

Donna Jay
Bartlesville, OK

Rosy Apples

This recipe is really good if you make homemade marshmallows to complement orchard-picked apples.

6 whole Jonathan apples,
   peeled and cored
2 cups water
½ cup sugar
4 T. red hot candies
Red food coloring
6 large marshmallows

Mix water, sugar and candy in large pan. Add red food coloring to desired color. Cook apples in this syrupy mixture until apples are tender. Move apples to a pie plate and pour syrup mix over apples. Place one large marshmallow on top of each apple. Set pan in 375°F oven until marshmallows are light brown.

Helen Tschanz
Harwood, MO

Cherry Pie

For this pie, prepare a pastry blended with nutmeg and grated orange peel.

Pie
2 cups fresh tart pie cherries,
   pitted, reserve juice
¼ tsp. cinnamon
½ cup sugar (or less)
1½ T. quick-cooking tapioca
1 can cherry pie filling

Topping
½ cup sugar
½ cup butter
1 cup flour

Heat oven to 400°F. Drain tart cherries, reserving ¼ cup of the liquid. Add cinnamon, sugar and tapioca to the cherry liquid. Combine the cherries, the liquid mixture and the cherry pie filling. Pour into 9- or 10-inch pie shell. Mix together the sugar, butter and flour for the crumb topping and sprinkle over top of pie. Bake for 35 to 45 minutes.

Sally Biszek
Coopersburg, PA

Aunt Frances' Angel Food Cake

A fresh fruit or berry mixture is a delicious accompaniment for angel food cake. Try a sauce of nectarine, blackberry and orange, or strawberry, blueberry and raspberry.

8 to 10 egg whites
4 T. water
Pinch of salt
1 tsp. cream of tartar (beat until
   stiff, not dry)
1½ cups sugar
1 tsp. vanilla
1 cup flour, sifted four times

Mix egg whites, water, salt and cream of tartar. Beat until frothy. Fold in sugar; then add vanilla and flour. Set in cold oven. Bake in a medium oven (310° to 320°F) for 10 minutes, then a slow oven (275°F) for 35 minutes and finally a medium oven (325°F) for the last 10 minutes. Stand the cake upside down for 1 hour. Loosen the edges to help slide the cake out.

Andie Rathbone
Dallas, TX

Baked Cheesecake

This cheesecake can be baked in a 10-inch springform pan or a 10-inch tart pan. Serve with fresh fruit.

Cheesecake

4-6 graham crackers, crushed

5 eggs, separated

1 cup sugar

2 (8-oz.) pkgs. cream cheese, softened

1 cup sour cream

2 T. flour

1 tsp. vanilla or lemon extract

Topping

1 cup sour cream

3½ T. sugar

1 tsp. vanilla or lemon extract

Heat oven to 275°F. Grease a 9 x 14-inch-long glass baking dish. Shake the graham cracker crumbs over the bottom of the dish and spread evenly. Set dish aside.

Beat egg yolks until thick and lemon colored. Gradually beat in sugar and add cream cheese, beating well until smooth. Add sour cream, flour and flavoring. Beat until smooth. In a separate bowl, beat egg whites until stiff and fold into cheese mixture. Pour this into the already prepared baking dish, spreading to even out. Bake 70 minutes. Turn oven off and leave cake in oven 1 hour without opening the door. Remove cake from oven and cool about 1 more hour.

To make topping, mix sour cream, sugar and flavoring. Spread on top of cake when cake has cooled. Cover frosted cake carefully with foil or plastic. Wrap foil or plastic tightly so that it doesn't drag into frosting. Refrigerate overnight or for several hours.

Mary Jane Smith
Brigham City, UT

desserts

145

"Red Dirt" Kauai Carrot Cake

This cake can be made in 8- or 9-inch round or square baking pans. It also can be made ahead and refrigerated overnight or frozen for 1 to 2 weeks.

Cake
4 eggs
1¼ cups oil
2 cups sugar
2 tsp. vanilla
2 cups flour
2 tsp. baking powder
1 tsp. baking soda
¼ tsp. salt
2½ tsp. cinnamon
2½ cups grated carrots
8 oz. can crushed
   pineapple, drained
½ cup flaked coconut
1 cup chopped walnuts

Butter Cream Frosting
½ cup butter, softened
8 oz. cream cheese (room temperature)
1 tsp. vanilla
3 cups sifted powdered sugar

Heat oven to 350°F. Beat together first four ingredients until blended. Beat in the next five ingredients until blended. Stir in remaining ingredients. Divide batter between two greased 9-inch tube pans and bake for about 40 minutes or until toothpick comes out clean. Frost when cool. Each cake serves 8 and recipe makes 2 cakes.

Beat butter and cream cheese until blended. Beat in remaining ingredients until smooth.

Judy Machorek
Melbourne, FL

White Chocolate Brownie Cake

Garnish this cake with white chocolate curls and a sprinkling of cocoa.

2 cups flour
2 cups sugar
1 tsp. baking soda
1 tsp. cinnamon (optional)
1 cup butter
1 cup water
⅓ cup white chocolate
2 eggs
1 tsp. vanilla
½ cup buttermilk

Frosting
½ cup butter
6 T. milk
⅓ cup white chocolate
1 lb. powdered sugar
1 cup chopped nuts

Heat oven to 400°F. In a large bowl, sift together flour, sugar, baking soda and cinnamon. In a large saucepan, melt together and boil the butter, water and white chocolate. Pour white chocolate mixture over the flour and sugar mixture. Add eggs, vanilla and buttermilk. Pour into a greased and floured 12 x 17-inch half sheet pan. Bake for about 30 minutes or until done.

Begin preparing frosting about 5 minutes before cake is done. Melt together butter, milk and white chocolate and bring to a boil. Add powdered sugar and nuts. Frost cake while still warm.

For a different flavor you can substitute 4 T. of cocoa powder for the white chocolate. Cut the baking time to 20 minutes.

Joseph Haughton
Coeur D'Alene, ID

Cranberry Pudding

This cranberry pudding is deliciously rich and elegantly presented in crystal dessert dishes. Glaze additional cranberries and sprinkle several over each serving.

Pudding

3 T. butter or margarine
1 cup sugar
2 cups flour
3 tsp. baking powder
Pinch of salt
1 cup milk
1 tsp. vanilla
1½ cups whole cranberries

Sauce

1 cup sugar
½ cup butter or margarine
¾ cup sweet cream

Heat oven to 350°F. Cream together butter and sugar. In a separate bowl, sift together flour, baking powder and salt. Add flour mixture to creamed mixture alternately with milk. Blend on low speed. Add vanilla and blend. Stir in cranberries by hand. Pour batter into greased 8 x 8-inch or 9 x 9-inch glass baking dish. Bake for 30 to 35 minutes, or until cake tests done (toothpick comes out clean).

To make sauce, combine sugar, butter and cream in a saucepan and bring to a boil. Pour over individual servings of pudding while sauce is still hot.

Charles A. Nicodemus
Walkersville, MD

Aunt Lil's Raisin Cookies

Make these cookies with sour pie, bing or maraschino cherries. Try making them with dried cherries, too; plump them in the water with the raisins.

2 cups raisins
1 cup cold water
1 tsp. baking soda
2 eggs
2 cups sugar
1 cup shortening
1 tsp. baking powder
½ tsp. cinnamon
1 tsp. vanilla
Dash of salt
3 cups flour
1 cup cherries, chopped and drained
1 cup walnuts, chopped

Place raisins in cold water, heat to boiling and boil for 5 minutes. Cool. Add baking soda and let stand a few minutes. Mix eggs, sugar, shortening, baking powder, cinnamon, vanilla, salt and flour. Add cherries and nuts. Let dough stand overnight.

Heat oven to 375°F. Drop dough by teaspoonfuls on greased cookie sheet and bake for approximately 12 minutes. (If raisins are too juicy, you can add another ½ to ¾ cup flour.)

Ruth Rines
Pittsfield,
ME

Index